THE OFFICIAL
LEEDS
UNITED
ANNUAL 2017

Written by Ryan Parrish

Designed by Mathew Whittles

A Grange Publication

© 2016. Published by Grange Communications Ltd., Edinburgh, under licence from Leeds United Football Club. Printed in the EU.

Every effort has been made to ensure the accuracy of information within this publication but the publishers cannot be held responsible for any errors or omissions. Views expressed are those of the author and do not necessarily represent those of the publishers or the football club. All rights reserved.

Photographs © Varley Picture Agency / Yorkshire Evening Post

ISBN 978-1-911287-07-0

WELCOME TO THE OFFICIAL LEEDS UNITED ANNUAL 2017!

As the start of another year draws in, we hope with everything crossed that the next 12 months include a return to the Promised Land for our beloved club.

2015/16 had its fleeting moments of joy and inspiration, but ultimately fell short of expectations and the challenge remains the same this time around.

In this Annual, we will be taking a closer look at those tasked with bringing Premier League football back to Elland Road for the first time in 13 years.

We also welcome Garry Monk to Leeds and get to know the boss who has vowed to bring entertaining football to LS11, profiling his impressive career to date within these pages.

Once you've delved deeper into the world of Leeds United, we have a number of quizzes and puzzles to put your knowledge to the test on all things white, yellow and blue. We hope you enjoy it.

Marching on Together!

CONTENTS

LEEDS UNITED HONOURS

FOOTBALL LEAGUE

1968-69 First Division champions

1973-74 First Division champions

1991-92 First Division champions

1923-24 Second Division champions

1963-64 Second Division champions

1989-90 Second Division champions

1927-28 Second Division runners-up

1931-32 Second Division runners-up

1955-56 Second Division runners-up

2009-10 League One runners-up

FA CUP

1972 FA Cup winners

1965 FA Cup finalists

1970 FA Cup finalists

1973 FA Cup finalists

FOOTBALL LEAGUE CUP

1968 Football League Cup winners

1996 Football League Cup finalists

CHARITY SHIELD

1969 FA Charity Shield winners

1992 FA Charity Shield winners

1974 FA Charity Shield runners-up

FA YOUTH CUP

1993 FA Youth Cup winners

1997 FA Youth Cup winners

EUROPEAN CUP

1974-75 European Cup finalists

EUROPEAN CUP WINNERS' CUP

1972-73 European Cup Winners' Cup finalists

INTER CITIES FAIRS CUP/UEFA CUP

1967-68 European Fairs Cup winners

1970-71 European Fairs Cup winners

1966-67 European Fairs Cup finalists

HIGHLIGHTS OF 2015/16

2015/16 proved to be another season of ups and downs for the Whites. Month by month, we take a look back at the last campaign and pick out some of the highlights along the way...

AUGUST

Results

Leeds United 1 (Antenucci 83)
Burnley 1 (Vokes 86)

Doncaster Rovers 1 (Williams pen 31)
Leeds United 1 (Cook 14)
League Cup (lost 2-4 on penalties)

Reading 0, Leeds United 0

Bristol City 2 (Agard 89, Flint 90+5)
Leeds United 2 (Antenucci pen 39, Wood 52)

Leeds United 1 (Wood 61)
Sheffield Wednesday 1 (Matias 37)

Derby County 1 (Martin 48)
Leeds United 2 (Adeyemi 43, Wood 88)

In ▶ Charlie Horton (Cardiff City), Lee Erwin (Motherwell), Sol Bamba (Palermo), Chris Wood (Leicester City), Tom Adeyemi (Cardiff City, loan), Ross Turnbull (Barnsley), Stuart Dallas (Brentford)

◀ Out Billy Sharp (Sheffield United), Steve Morison (Millwall), Nick Ajose (Swindon Town)

Highlights

vs Burnley (1-1 draw)
Saturday August 8, 2015
Elland Road

Following a summer which included the appointment of head coach Uwe Rosler and the signings of Chris Wood, Stuart Dallas and Sol Bamba among others, United's 2015/16 campaign got underway with an enthralling 1-1 draw at home to newly-relegated Burnley. Mirco Antenucci opened the scoring to raise the roof at Elland Road after 83 minutes, netting a sensational curling effort which looked to put the hosts on course for a winning start, only for former United loanee Sam Vokes to head home an equaliser three minutes later.

vs Derby County (2-1 win)
Saturday August 29, 2015
iPro Stadium

Despite exiting the Capital One Cup on penalties at Doncaster Rovers five days on from the opening day draw with Burnley, United remained unbeaten in the league during the early weeks of the season but were made to wait until the final weekend of August to secure their first three points. They came in dramatic fashion too, with Chris Wood thundering an 88th-minute winner in off the post after promotion hopefuls Derby had pulled themselves level to cancel out a towering header from on-loan midfielder Tom Adeyemi.

SEPTEMBER

Results

Leeds United 1 (Antenucci 76)
Brentford 1 (Djuricin 29)

Leeds United 0
Ipswich Town 1 (Smith 32)

MK Dons 1 (Church 74)
Leeds United 2 (Wood pen 31, Taylor 43)

Middlesbrough 3 (Nugent 3, Bellusci OG 32, Fabbrini 81)
Leeds United 0

In ▶ Jordan Botaka (Excelsior)

Highlights

vs MK Dons (2-1 win)
Saturday September 19, 2015
Stadium mk

United returned from the season's first international break to record a 1-1 draw with Brentford before slipping to a first Championship defeat of the campaign at home to Ipswich Town. Amends were made the following weekend, though, as a Charlie Taylor-inspired performance secured the three points in front of 6,297 travelling fans. Taylor's lung-busting run drew the penalty for Wood to open the scoring at Stadium mk, before the full-back netted his first senior goal for the club with a precise strike into the bottom corner.

OCTOBER

Results

Leeds United 0,
Birmingham City 2 (Gray 31, Maghoma 90+1)

Leeds United 1 (Cooper 22)
Brighton & Hove Albion 2 (March 14, Zamora 89)

Fulham 1 (Dembele 23)
Leeds United 1 (Wood pen 64)

Bolton Wanderers 1 (Ameobi 32)
Leeds United 1 (Antenucci pen 71)

Leeds United 0,
Blackburn Rovers 2 (Conway 1, Rhodes 6)

In ▶ Will Buckley (Sunderland, loan)

◀ Out Lee Erwin (Bury, loan)

NOVEMBER

||||||||||||||||||||||||||||||||||||||||||||||||||||||||||||||||||

Results

Leeds United 1 (Mowatt 63)
Cardiff City 0

Huddersfield Town 0
Leeds United 3 (Antenucci 45+5, Wood 45+7, Mowatt 54)

Leeds United 0
Rotherham United 1 (Newell 54)

Queens Park Rangers 1 (Austin 58)
Leeds United 0

In ▶ Liam Bridcutt (Sunderland, loan)

◀ Out Ross Killock (Stockport County, loan), Will
Buckley (Sunderland, loan terminated), Charlie
Horton (mutual consent)

Highlights

vs Cardiff City (1-0 win)
Tuesday November 3, 2015
Elland Road

United endured a winless October and, after 12 games
in charge, Rosler was replaced by former Rotherham
boss Steve Evans, who oversaw draws at Fulham and
Bolton before suffering defeat at home to Blackburn
in his first three matches. His fourth game at the helm
however, a midweek visit of Cardiff City, saw United
end an eight-month wait for victory on home soil
courtesy of a trademark Alex Mowatt thunderbolt.
Mowatt struck just after the hour mark to secure
United's first win over the Bluebirds in 31 years.

vs Huddersfield Town (3-0 win)
Saturday November 7, 2015
John Smith's Stadium

Four days on from the uplifting victory against Cardiff,
United made it back-to-back wins for the first time all
season with an emphatic Yorkshire derby demolition of
Huddersfield Town. After a cagey opening 45 minutes
at the John Smith's Stadium, quick-fire goals from
Antenucci and Wood deep into first-half stoppage
time suddenly gave Evans' side a comfortable lead
going into the break. Mowatt then hit his second
wonder-strike in as many matches shortly after the
restart to wrap up a fourth consecutive win over
United's nearest Championship rivals.

DECEMBER

Results

Leeds United 2 (Wood 30, Adeyemi 45)
Hull City 1 (Elmohamady 51)

Charlton Athletic 0
Leeds United 0

Wolverhampton Wanderers 2 (Afobe 10, Byrne 81)
Leeds United 3 (Byram 44 & 60, Dallas 51)

Leeds United 1 (Browne OG 46)
Preston North End 0

Nottingham Forest 1 (Oliveira 17)
Leeds United 1 (Byram 80)

Leeds United 2 (Bamba 42, Wood 71)
Derby County 2 (Hendrick 13, Ince 78)

Highlights

vs Hull City (2-1 win)
Saturday December 5, 2015
Elland Road

Consecutive defeats to Rotherham and Queens Park Rangers dampened the derby joys of Huddersfield, but United bounced back by embarking on an unbeaten December which saw the team climb the Championship table, starting with an impressive victory at home to high-flying Hull City. Adeyemi and Wood were on target during a dominant first half to take a deserved two-goal cushion into the break, before Ahmed Elmohamady pulled one back in the second half to set up a nervy finale, with United forced to withstand plenty of Hull pressure.

vs Wolverhampton Wanderers (3-2 win)
Thursday December 17, 2015
Molineux Stadium

A goalless draw at Charlton followed the win over Hull, before United headed to Stadium for a televised midweek clash which saw Sam Byram mark his return to the team in spectacular fashion. Byram, who would join Premier League side West Ham the following month, slotted home on the stroke of half-time to cancel out Benik Afobe's opener. Stuart Dallas then rifled in his first goal for the club before Byram netted his second of the evening with a towering header. Wolves pulled one back but Leeds held firm.

JANUARY

Results

Leeds United 1 (Kay OG 87)
MK Dons 1 (Hall 30)

Leeds United 2 (Carayol 45, Doukara 90)
Rotherham United 0
FA Cup Third Round

Ipswich Town 2 (Chambers 50, Pitman 90+2)
Leeds United 1 (Doukara 1)

Sheffield Wednesday 2 (Hooper 47 & 50)
Leeds United 0

Leeds United 1 (Doukara 59)
Bristol City 0

Brentford 1 (Saunders 27)
Leeds United 1 (Carayol 84)

Bolton Wanderers 1 (Pratley 80),
Leeds United 2 (Doukara 9, Diagouraga 39)
FA Cup Fourth Round

In ▶ Mustapha Carayol (Middlesbrough, loan),
Toumani Diagouraga (Brentford), Jack McKay
(Doncaster Rovers), Paul McKay (Doncaster Rovers)

◀ Out Sam Byram (West Ham United), Robbie
McDaid (Lincoln City, loan), Tommaso Bianchi (Ascoli,
loan), Chris Dawson (Rotherham United)

Highlights

vs Bolton Wanderers (2–1 win)
FA Cup Fourth Round
Saturday January 30, 2016
Macron Stadium

United made a mixed start to the new year but a 2-0
FA Cup victory at home to Rotherham teed up this
Fourth Round trip to the Macron Stadium. In-form
Souleymane Doukara netted his fourth goal in six
matches to open the scoring after just nine minutes,
before full debutant Toumani Diagouraga – signed
from Brentford at the start of the week – doubled
the advantage with a composed finish shortly before
half-time. United's progression was sealed, despite
the hosts grabbing a consolation goal late on.

FEBRUARY

Results

Leeds United 0
Nottingham Forest 1 (Oliveira 60)

Leeds United 0
Middlesbrough 0

Watford 1 (Wootton OG 54)
Leeds United 0
FA Cup Fifth Round

Leeds United 1 (Cook 38)
Fulham 1 (Cairney 17)

Brighton & Hove Albion 4 (Hemed pen 18 & 28,
Cooper OG 22, Dunk 38)
Leeds United 0

MARCH

Results

Leeds United 2 (Antenucci 39 & 62)
Bolton Wanderers 1 (Woolery 74)

Cardiff City 0
Leeds United 2 (Doukara 37, Antenucci 90+4)

Blackburn Rovers 1 (Jackson 89)
Leeds United 2 (Bamba 34, Antenucci 69)

Leeds United 1 (Dallas 22)
Huddersfield Town 4 (Hudson 41, Bunn 69, Matmour 73, Wells 77)

◀ **Out** Luke Parkin (mutual consent)

Highlights

vs Cardiff City (2-0 win)
Tuesday March 8, 2016
Cardiff City Stadium

February passed without victory and United owed a response to the travelling fans who witnessed a humiliating 4-0 defeat at Brighton. Bolton were beaten 2-1 at Elland Road the following Saturday, before Evans' side truly made amends by clinching an unexpected seasonal double over Cardiff in South Wales. Doukara was back among the goals, firing United ahead after 37 minutes, but the three points owed plenty to the heroics of Marco Silvestri, who kept the visitors in it before Antenucci wrapped things up in stoppage time.

APRIL

Results

Rotherham United 2 (Frecklington 27, Halford pen 90)
Leeds United 1 (Murphy 79)

Leeds United 1 (Wood 70)
Queens Park Rangers 1 (Chery pen 87)

Burnley 1 (Arfield 1)
Leeds United 0

Birmingham City 1 (Donaldson 53)
Leeds United 2 (Dallas 11 & 50)

Leeds United 3 (Diagouraga 48, Wood 69 & 85)
Reading 2 (Hector 39, Rakels 81)

Leeds United 2 (Bamba 60, Diagouraga 64)
Wolverhampton Wanderers 1 (Saville 77)

Hull City 2 (Hernandez 45+1, Huddlestone 45+3)
Leeds United 2 (Wood 15, Dallas 88)

Leeds United 1 (Bamba 71)
Charlton Athletic 2 (Gudmundsson 39, Lookman 49)

Highlights

vs Birmingham City (2-1 win)
Tuesday April 12, 2016
St Andrew's Stadium

United's rearranged trip to the West Midlands came on the back of a four-game winless run, but their dominant display in a harsh 1-0 defeat at eventual champions Burnley the previous Saturday suggested their fortunes could be about to turn. Dallas was in inspired form to ensure that would be the case at St Andrew's, hitting an impressive brace – including a Goal of the Season contender in the second half – before Birmingham threatened a fightback, with Clayton Donaldson on target for the hosts shortly after United's second.

vs Reading (3-2 win)
Saturday April 16, 2016
Elland Road

The victory over Birmingham set United up for an encouraging end to the campaign, with Evans' side putting another three points on the board when former Leeds boss Brian McDermott brought his Reading team to Elland Road. A five-goal thriller saw the hosts fall behind in the first half before turning the game on its head courtesy of efforts from Diagouraga and Wood. The Royals managed to pull themselves back on level terms, but Wood had the final say with his second goal of the afternoon five minutes from time.

2015/16 Leeds United top appearance makers:

Stuart Dallas (49)
Marco Silvestri (48)
Lewis Cook (47)
Charlie Taylor (43)
Mirco Antenucci (43)
Liam Cooper (41)

Highlights

vs Preston North End
Saturday May 7, 2016
Deepdale

Having suffered defeat to relegated Charlton in their final home game of the season a week earlier, United's campaign was brought to a close with a 1-1 draw away to Simon Grayson's Preston North End. Wood dispatched a second-half penalty to take his tally to 13 for the season and put the visitors in front, but Preston snatched a point in stoppage-time through substitute Jordan Hugill's close-range finish. A share of the spoils meant United finished 2015/16 in 13th – two places higher than the previous year.

MAY

Results

Preston North End 1 (Hugill 90+2)
Leeds United 1 (Wood pen 78)

◀ **Out** Mirco Antenucci, Scott Wootton, Lewis Walters, Eric Grimes, Ross Killock, Jake Skelton, Robbie McDaid, Tom Lyman (all released)

2015/16 Leeds United top goalscorers:

Chris Wood (13)   Mirco Antenucci (9)
Stuart Dallas (5)   Souleymane Doukara (5)
Sol Bamba (4)

Final 2015/16 Championship table

Pos	Team	P	Home					Away					GD	Pts
			W	D	L	GF	GA	W	D	L	GF	GA		
1	Burnley	46	15	6	2	38	14	11	9	3	34	21	37	93
2	Middlesbrough	46	16	5	2	34	8	10	6	7	29	23	32	89
3	Brighton	46	15	5	3	40	18	9	12	2	32	24	30	89
4	Hull	46	15	7	1	47	12	9	4	10	22	23	34	83
5	Derby	46	12	7	4	37	16	9	8	6	29	27	23	78
6	Sheff Wed	46	13	8	2	42	17	6	9	8	24	28	21	74
7	Ipswich	46	9	8	6	28	24	9	7	7	25	27	2	69
8	Cardiff	46	12	9	2	33	20	5	8	10	23	31	5	68
9	Brentford	46	10	4	9	33	30	9	4	10	39	37	5	65
10	Birmingham	46	9	5	9	27	27	7	10	6	26	22	4	63
11	Preston	46	7	10	6	21	21	8	7	8	24	24	0	62
12	QPR	46	10	9	4	37	25	4	9	10	17	29	0	60
13	Leeds	46	7	8	8	23	28	7	9	7	27	30	-8	59
14	Wolves	46	7	10	6	26	26	7	6	10	27	32	-5	58
15	Blackburn	46	8	8	7	29	23	5	8	10	17	23	0	55
16	Nottm Forest	46	7	8	8	25	26	6	8	9	18	21	-4	55
17	Reading	46	8	9	6	25	20	5	4	14	27	39	-7	52
18	Bristol City	46	7	7	9	34	34	6	6	11	20	37	-17	52
19	Huddersfield	46	7	6	10	33	33	6	6	11	26	37	-11	51
20	Fulham	46	8	5	10	36	36	4	10	9	30	43	-13	51
21	Rotherham	46	8	6	9	31	34	5	4	14	22	37	-18	49
22	Charlton	46	5	8	10	23	35	4	5	14	17	45	-40	40
23	MK Dons	46	7	3	13	21	37	2	9	12	18	32	-30	39
24	Bolton	46	5	11	7	24	26	0	4	19	17	55	-40	30

GOALKEEPERS

ROB GREEN

D.O.B.: 18/01/1980 | **NATIONALITY:** English

The former England international was snapped up by Garry Monk on a one-year deal over the summer, shortly after his release from Championship rivals Queens Park Rangers.

Green, a vastly-experienced 'keeper who arrived at Elland Road with over 600 career appearances to his name, progressed through the ranks at Norwich City and enjoyed a six-year stint at West Ham United before joining QPR in 2012.

Green, 36 at the time of putting pen to paper, immediately became the oldest member of the first-team squad upon signing for Leeds back in July and was handed the number 1 shirt in time for the new campaign.

ROSS TURNBULL

D.O.B.: 04/01/1985 | **NATIONALITY:** English

Signed from Barnsley in summer 2015 to provide competition for United's number 1 shirt, the former Middlesbrough and Chelsea man endured a frustrating debut season at Elland Road.

Turnbull was restricted to just one senior appearance last term – coming in a League Cup tie at Doncaster Rovers – after a broken ankle, sustained in a behind-close-doors friendly at Thorp Arch, saw him sidelined for the majority of the campaign.

Turnbull, who is capped by England at Under-19s level and has a Champions League winner's medal to his name, is under contract at Elland Road until the summer.

MARCO SILVESTRI

D.O.B.: 02/03/1991 | **NATIONALITY:** Italian

The agile shot-stopper, a summer 2014 arrival from Serie A side Chievo, missed just one Championship fixture last season.

Silvestri, who has previously represented Italy at Under-21s level, began his career with homeland side Modena before joining Chievo and enjoying loan spells with Reggiana, Padova and Cagliari – the club previously owned by United chairman Massimo Cellino.

After switching to Elland Road on a four-year deal, Silvestri was shortlisted for United's Player of the Year award during his debut season in English football and continues to earn rave reviews between the sticks.

BAILEY PEACOCK-FARRELL

D.O.B.: 29/10/96 | **NATIONALITY:** English

The youngster found himself unexpectedly thrown into the first-team fold last season following injury to Turnbull and the departure of Charlie Horton, but Peacock-Farrell proved an able deputy to Silvestri when handed his senior debut.

The Darlington-born stopper, who joined United from Middlesbrough's Academy in 2013, stepped in for the suspended Silvestri for the visit of Queens Park Rangers and was beaten only by a late penalty in a 1-1 draw.

One year on from signing his first professional contract with the club, Peacock-Farrell penned a new two-year deal at Elland Road over the summer after reportedly attracting Premier League interest.

DEFENDERS

LIAM COOPER

D.O.B.: 30/08/1991 | **NATIONALITY:** Scottish

United's vice-captain made the switch to Elland Road from Chesterfield in summer 2014 after catching the eye in a pre-season friendly against the Whites.

Cooper, a product of Hull City's Academy, has been a regular fixture at the heart of the United defence since his arrival and earned a call-up to the senior Scotland squad for the first time last season.

The left-sided centre-back previously spent time on loan at Carlisle United and Huddersfield Town while on the books of Hull, before earning a place in the League Two PFA Team of the Year 2013/14 as he helped Chesterfield secure promotion.

PONTUS JANSSON

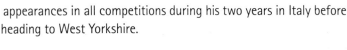

D.O.B.: 13/02/1991 | **NATIONALITY:** Swedish

The Swedish international joined United on a season-long loan from Italian outfit Torino during the second week of the current campaign.

Jansson, a towering six-foot-five centre-back who was part of Sweden's Euro 2016 squad, began his career with homeland side Malmo FF, where he worked under United assistant boss Pep Clotet and won three league titles.

The defender made the switch to Serie A in 2014 and made 25 appearances in all competitions during his two years in Italy before heading to West Yorkshire.

KYLE BARTLEY

D.O.B.: 22/05/1991 | **NATIONALITY: English**

Monk's second signing of the summer saw the United boss reunited with a familiar face as Swansea City centre-back Kyle Bartley arrived on a season-long loan.

Bartley, a former England Under-17s international, played alongside and worked under Monk during his time at the Liberty Stadium after joining from Arsenal in 2012.

The Stockport-born defender, who won the FA Youth Cup and featured in the Champions League during his time with Arsenal, has enjoyed loan spells with Sheffield United, Rangers and Birmingham City in recent years.

GAETANO BERARDI

D.O.B.: 21/08/1988 | **NATIONALITY: Swiss**

The Swiss full-back, signed from Italian outfit Sampdoria in July 2014, is rapidly earning cult hero status at Elland Road for his commitment to the cause in the face of several injury setbacks.

Berardi, who is equally as comfortable playing on the right or the left, endured a testing start to life in English football and was sent off on his United debut, but the defender's solid performances have established him as a key figure in the side and earned him a Player of the Year nomination last season.

Berardi twice won the play-offs during his time in Serie B, with Brescia and Sampdoria.

CHARLIE TAYLOR

D.O.B.: 18/09/1993 | **NATIONALITY: English**

The Thorp Arch graduate capped a fine 2015/16 season by collecting United's Player of the Year award, despite missing a chunk of the campaign through illness.

The York-born full-back, who progressed through the ranks to make his debut as a 17-year-old in 2011, was made to be patient for a regular run in the United side and spent time on loan at Bradford City, York City, Inverness and Fleetwood Town, prior to making the left-back spot his own at the start of 2015.

Taylor, capped by England at Under-19s level, is regarded as one of the brightest prospects in the Championship.

LEWIE COYLE

D.O.B.: 15/10/1995 | **NATIONALITY:** English

The Hull-born full-back has been on United's books since the age of seven and eventually made his first-team debut last season after impressing as captain of the Under-21s.

Coyle, who had a brief loan spell at Harrogate Town in 2014, made his first outing as a late substitute away to Nottingham Forest before being handed a first start at home to Rotherham United in the FA Cup. He went on to end the campaign with 13 appearances to his name.

The Academy product comes from a particularly sporting family, with eldest brother Tommy a professional boxer and second-eldest, Joe, a professional golfer.

LUKE AYLING

D.O.B.: 25/08/1991 | **NATIONALITY:** English

A product of Arsenal's youth system, the versatile defender arrived at Elland Road over the summer following two impressive seasons with Championship rivals Bristol City.

Ayling, who signed a three-year deal with United in August, went straight into Garry Monk's starting line-up and was named Man of the Match following his debut against Birmingham City.

Mainly a right-back throughout his career, Ayling spent four years with Yeovil Town and helped the Glovers achieve promotion from League One before making the switch to Ashton Gate.

MIDFIELDERS

EUNAN O'KANE

D.O.B.: 10/07/1990 | **NATIONALITY:** Irish

The Republic of Ireland international became our 11th and final signing of the summer 2016 transfer window when he arrived on deadline day on a two-year deal from AFC Bournemouth.

O'Kane, who spent time with Everton's Academy as a youngster, made 16 Premier League appearances last season having enjoyed a rise through the divisions in his career so far.

The midfielder joined Bournemouth, then a League One side, from Torquay United in 2012 and helped the Cherries go on to achieve top-flight promotion, making over 100 appearances, during his four-year stay on the South Coast.

LUKE MURPHY

D.O.B.: 21/10/1989 | **NATIONALITY:** English

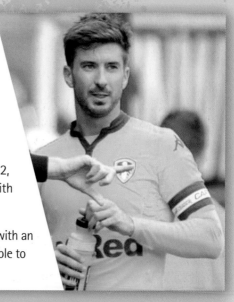

The summer 2013 signing from Crewe Alexandra is one of United's longest-serving players and entered the new season as the top appearance maker within the current squad.

Murphy, who helped fire Crewe to promotion from League Two in 2012, wasted little time in introducing himself to the Elland Road faithful with a dramatic late winner on his United debut.

The Macclesfield-born midfielder missed the early parts of last season with an injury sustained at the start of the summer and, as a result, he was unable to nail down a regular place in the side for large parts of the campaign.

TOUMANI DIAGOURAGA

D.O.B.: 09/06/1987 | **NATIONALITY:** Malian

After signing from Championship rivals Brentford in January 2016, the former Paris Saint-Germain trainee made his United debut away to the Bees just one day after completing his switch from Griffin Park.

Diagouraga, whose career in English football began at Watford, ended last season with three goals to his name after waiting almost three years since last finding the net. He arrived at Elland Road on a two-and-a-half-year deal not long after being named the Brentford Supporters' Player of the Season.

The Paris-born central-midfielder has been in England for 12 years now and has also had stints at Swindon, Rotherham, Hereford, Peterborough and Portsmouth.

STUART DALLAS

D.O.B.: 19/04/1991 | **NATIONALITY:** Northern Irish

The Northern Ireland international soon settled into life at Elland Road following his summer 2015 move from Brentford, ending his debut campaign as United's Players' Player of the Year after being crowned by his team-mates.

Dallas, who began his career with semi-professional homeland side Crusaders, earning just £70 a week, became the first United player to feature in a major tournament for 10 years when he represented his country at Euro 2016.

The winger, a League One promotion winner with Brentford in 2014, netted five goals last term, including an impressive double away to Birmingham and a late equaliser at Hull.

KALVIN PHILLIPS

D.O.B.: 02/12/1995 | **NATIONALITY:** English

The homegrown central-midfielder scored on his Elland Road debut – a 2-1 defeat to Cardiff City in April 2015 – just five days after making his first senior appearance away to Wolverhampton Wanderers.

Phillips, who joined the club from local side Wortley Juniors in 2010, progressed through the ranks at Thorp Arch and earned a glowing reputation for his all-action displays prior to his first-team breakthrough.

The youngster still featured regularly with the Under-21s last season, though, as he was limited to just 10 Championship appearances in total, with his only three starts coming during the opening month of the campaign.

MATT GRIMES

D.O.B.: 15/07/1995 | **NATIONALITY:** English

The England Under-21s international followed Swansea teammate Bartley in making a season-long loan switch to Elland Road over the summer.

Grimes, originally signed by Monk in early 2015 after catching the eye with hometown club Exeter City, has a handful of Premier League appearances to his name and spent time on loan in the Championship with Blackburn Rovers last season.

The central midfielder, who is seen as a set-piece specialist, joined United with the intention of getting regular first-team football under his belt and adding to his international honours with England's youth teams.

LIAM BRIDCUTT

D.O.B.: 08/05/1989 | **NATIONALITY:** Scottish

The Scotland international rejoined United permanently last summer on the back of a successful loan spell from Sunderland in 2015/16.

Bridcutt, a product of Chelsea's Academy, was shortlisted for United's Player of the Year award after making a big impression in his 27 appearances in all competitions while on loan at Elland Road.

The central midfielder made his name during a four-year stint with Brighton and earned a Premier League switch to Sunderland in January 2014. Bridcutt penned a two-year deal at Elland Road in August.

PABLO HERNANDEZ

D.O.B.: 11/04/1985 | **NATIONALITY:** Spanish

A Spanish international with over 130 La Liga appearances to his name, the former Swansea City winger became United's seventh summer signing when he joined on loan from Qatari side Al-Arabi.

The experienced Hernandez, who played alongside and worked under Monk during his recent two-year stint at the Liberty Stadium, moved to Elland Road for an initial six-month spell with the option of making his stay permanent.

Hernandez progressed through Valencia's famed youth system and joined Swansea for a then club-record fee in 2012.

ALEX MOWATT

D.O.B.: 13/02/1995 | **NATIONALITY:** English

The Doncaster-born midfielder, another graduate of United's famed Thorp Arch Academy, is renowned for beating Championship goal-keepers from distance with stunning strikes with his deadly left foot.

Mowatt was the club's Player of the Year for 2014/15 and has earned international recognition with England Under-20s, although he often found himself in and out of the United starting line-up last season.

The last campaign saw Mowatt, who first joined his boyhood club aged nine, reach a century of league appearances and score arguably his finest goals in Leeds colours – against Cardiff City and Huddersfield Town – both in the space of four days.

RONALDO VIEIRA

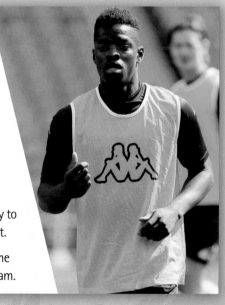

D.O.B.: 20/07/1998 | **NATIONALITY:** Guinea-Bissau (although eligible to play for Portugal)

Born in Guinea-Bissau, but having grown up in Portugal and spent time on the books of European giants Benfica, the highly-rated youngster first arrived at United on trial in 2015 after catching the eye playing for York College.

Vieira, who moved to England with his family in 2011, was thrown into the spotlight during the final week of last season, making his senior debut away to Preston North End just two days after signing his first professional contract.

The central midfielder started 2015/16 as a first-year scholar playing in the Under-18s, but he soon progressed to the Under-21s and into the first team.

KEMAR ROOFE

D.O.B.: 06/01/1993 | **NATIONALITY:** English

Monk bolstered his attacking options by swooping for last season's League Two Player of the Year on a four-year deal from Oxford United back in July.

Roofe, a former West Brom trainee, established himself as one of the Football League's hottest properties during 2015/16 as he helped fire his side to promotion with 26 goals from 49 appearances.

The versatile forward, who played alongside Wood during his time in West Brom's youth system, has previously spent time on loan at Icelandic side Vikingur Reykjavik, as well as homeland clubs Northampton Town, Cheltenham Town and Colchester United.

FORWARDS

HADI SACKO

D.O.B.: 24/03/1994 | **NATIONALITY:** French

Capped by France at Under-20s level, the pacy winger began his career with Bordeaux but was poached by Portuguese giants Sporting Lisbon in 2014.

Sacko, who returned to France last season for a stint with Ligue 2 outfit Sochaux, joined United over the summer on a season-long loan with a view to a permanent deal.

The youngster is yet to feature for Sporting's senior team but has featured over 50 times for their 'B' team. It took Sacko just 13 minutes to score in his first appearance in United colours – a pre-season friendly away to Irish side Shelbourne.

CHRIS WOOD

D.O.B.: 07/12/1991 | **NATIONALITY:** New Zealander

The New Zealand international ended his debut season at Elland Road as United's top goalscorer, finding the net 13 times in 2015/16 following his summer arrival from eventual Premier League champions Leicester City.

Wood, who is the youngest-ever player to captain his country, has achieved promotion with three of his previous clubs – West Brom, Brighton and Leicester. Penning a four-year deal with United saw the centre-forward become the club's most expensive signing outside of the top-flight.

Wood's senior career began with homeland side Cambridge FC, making his debut aged 15, before being brought to England by West Brom back in 2009.

MARCUS ANTONSSON

D.O.B.: 08/05/1991 | **NATIONALITY:** Swedish

United's first signing of summer 2016 arrived from Swedish outfit Kalmar FF on a three-year deal to end weeks of speculation linking him with a move to the Championship.

Antonsson, who was the Swedish top-flight's leading goalscorer at the time of his switch to Elland Road, previously worked under assistant coach Pep Clotet during his time with homeland side Halmstads BK.

The striker enjoyed a prolific run of 22 goals from 40 matches prior to joining United, and Antonsson marked his first start for his new club with a brace in a pre-season friendly victory over Shamrock Rovers in Ireland.

SOULEYMANE DOUKARA

D.O.B.: 29/09/1991 | **NATIONALITY:** Senegalese

The French forward, who is eligible to play for Senegal due to his parents, moved to United from Italian side Catania in summer 2014, with his initial loan switch made permanent after just two months in England.

Doukara, a trialist with AC Milan as a youngster, enjoyed a rich vein of form in front of goal at the start of 2016, netting four times from six matches, including the quickest of the season – after just 12 seconds – in a 2-1 defeat away to Ipswich Town.

The striker was suspended for eight games towards the end of last term for biting Fulham's Fernando Amorebieta.

MEET THE BOSS

Garry Monk

Date of birth: 06/03/1979

Birthplace: Bedford, England

Playing career: Torquay United, Southampton, Stockport County, Oxford United, Sheffield Wednesday, Barnsley, Swansea City

Playing position: Central defender

Teams managed:
Swansea City, Leeds United

Twitter: @GarryMonk

"I haven't come here to do the average or be mediocre," was Garry Monk's rallying call following last June's appointment as the new man in charge of Leeds United. "The Premier League is what we are here for and we can't shy away from that."

His opening words were bold but Monk's ambition has been evident throughout a career which has spanned from playing in League Two to becoming a Premier League manager at the age of just 34 – the division's youngest at the time.

"I'm a young manager but I'm not a manager that wants to take the easy route," he claimed. "I want to have challenges put in front of me – and big challenges."

Monk embraced a number of sizeable challenges during his 11-and-a-half-year association with Swansea City, with the South Wales outfit playing in League Two but plotting a rise through the divisions at the time of the defender's arrival from Barnsley back in 2004. Fast forward seven remarkable years, and Swansea's 2010/11 campaign culminated in Monk skippering the side to Premier League promotion via a Play-Off final victory at Wembley.

Two-and-a-half top-flight seasons later, and still the club captain, Monk was tasked with stepping in as player-manager and halting Swansea's perilous slide towards the relegation zone following the departure of Michael Laudrup.

Safety was secured with two games to spare and Monk's impact in the hot-seat prompted Swansea to offer the centre-back the job on a permanent basis, handing him a three-year deal. The Swans' faith in Monk was rewarded the following season as he led the club to a highest-ever Premier League finish of eighth with a record points tally of 56.

It was an achievement which led to links to the England job and another new contract at the Liberty Stadium. Expectations were high heading into

2015/16 but Swansea struggled to recreate the fine form of the previous campaign as results slipped, and Monk was relieved of his duties shortly before Christmas.

A brief spell out of the game followed, with Monk spending his time visiting a number of clubs across Europe, including Europa League champions Sevilla, to gain new ideas and insight in preparation for his next challenge. That would come six months on from his Swansea exit as a new era began at Elland Road.

"We all know the history of the club and the standing it has in English football," said Monk in his opening press conference. "The passion of the fans, the history and the ambition of the owner all ties in with what I wanted to do. I want to be challenged and really get my teeth into a big project. That was the underlying factor throughout the whole process and that's the reason why I'm here today."

BACKROOM STAFF

Pep Clotet
Assistant coach

James Beattie
First-team coach

Darryl Flahavan
Goalkeeping coach

GETTING TO KNOW YOU

We spoke to members of the Leeds United squad to find out what makes the players tick and uncover some interesting facts about their life on and off the pitch...

Lewie Coyle

Tell us about your remarkable sporting family...

"There are four brothers – Tommy is the eldest, he's a professional boxer and he's achieved a lot already. Then there's Joe who's trying to make his way in the professional golfing game, there's myself here at Leeds and then our youngest brother, Rocco, he's torn between football and boxing. He's playing at Hull City's Academy and boxing at Tommy's gym."

Chris Wood

Were you good at any sports other than football when you were growing up?

"I played a bit of cricket and rugby and was okay at them both. But I'd grown up loving football and I really enjoyed it. When I first moved to England, the football here did take some getting used to as it's so much bigger than in New Zealand."

Pablo Hernandez

Who was your footballing idol when you were growing up?

"Michael Laudrup when he was playing for Barcelona and Real Madrid. I always bought shirts – from Barcelona to Ajax – with his name on the back. I'm a lucky man because I was able to play for him for a year with Getafe in Spain and nearly two years at Swansea."

Kemar Roofe

What would you be if you weren't a footballer?

"Probably something in business, whether that's with property, cars or doing my clothing line with my brother."

Alex Mowatt

Who is the cleverest player in the squad?

"I don't think there are too many, to be honest! But I'll say Woodsy because he sounds quite posh!"

Hadi Sacko

Who is your best mate in the Leeds United squad?

"I grew up in the same building as Toumani Diagouraga in the suburbs of Paris. I was on the second floor and he was on the fourth floor until Toums left to go to Watford. He used to come back quite often so we saw each other quite a lot even when he was playing in England."

Marcus Antonsson

Tell us something interesting about your birthplace...

"Where I come from in Sweden, it's out in the forest a little bit and maybe one or two thousand people live there. But a lot of them are Leeds fans! It's a place called Unnaryd, it's located in the forest a little bit – a little village. A lot of people out there are happy that I came to Leeds!"

Rob Green

What song did you choose for your 'initiation' when you first joined the club?

"Girls and Boys by Blur, which, amazingly, I soon realised that no one knew because they're a lot younger than me! When I say I sung it, I shouted it – one verse, one chorus and I was out! I was glad to get my song out of the way."

UNITED IN IRELAND

reparations for the 2016/17 campaign truly kicked-off with two-week stay in Ireland, where United played their first re-season friendlies of the summer and enjoyed a vital eriod of team bonding with Garry Monk's summer signings.

TRAINING

The squad spent a fortnight training at the FAI's impressive Abbotstown HQ on the outskirts of Dublin, often spending their days working on double sessions and utilising the nearby gym and pool facilities. The two weeks spent together provided the perfect opportunity for Garry Monk and his coaching team to start implementing their new ideas, both physically and tactically, as they began to look towards August's season-opener away to Queens Park Rangers.

Assistant boss Pep Clotet explained: "All of the training sessions were designed to keep the players progressing and to take them forward. It was always based on the idea that we have for Leeds and the direction we want to go in. The facilities were fantastic and the set-up was unbelievable. It was a very good place to work because it was calm and we could focus. We also had fantastic resources at the hotel."

TEAM BONDING

Pre-season tours are traditionally prime time for team bonding exercises and United's summer trip to Ireland was no different, with the players and staff spending a day clay pigeon shooting at Courtlough Shooting Grounds in Balbriggan.

Once small-sided teams had been created, the group headed off to test their aim against a range of moving targets throughout the day, providing the new signings with the perfect opportunity to integrate with their new teammates away from the training pitch.

"I always find it important that we do some activities outside of the football," said Garry Monk. "It's something I'm very big on. It was a chance for the lads to have a bit of competition – you see a different side to their character and it's a good way to get them bonding outside of that football environment."

MEETING A LEGEND

One of the highlights of the pre-season tour came on the final day of training – when United and Ireland legend Johnny Giles paid the players and staff a special visit. Giles, who won two First Division titles, the FA Cup and League Cup among other silverware during his 12 years as a player at Elland Road, stopped by to chat to Garry Monk and his squad, before posing for photos with the team.

"It's great to come down and meet everyone", said Giles. "Leeds United was my club – I had great times during my 12 years there and it's nice to see them over in Dublin. I've got a few friends who are involved around this particular training centre and it's always nice to see the lads. I was just surprised they remembered me – they wouldn't have seen me playing as it was a long time ago! But they all seem like nice lads and Garry's a lovely chap – I had a nice chat with him and wished him all the best for the season."

MATCHES

Two friendly fixtures were played during United's time in Ireland and both ended in victory for Garry Monk's side.

First up were second division side Shelbourne, who welcomed around 2,500 supporters to Tolka Park to witness United's pre-season campaign get underway with a 2-1 win. Early goals from Souleymane Doukara and Hadi Sacko gave the visitors a comfortable lead, but Shelbourne pulled one back shortly after half-time to make it more of a contest.

United then travelled to Tallaght Stadium to face Irish top-flight outfit Shamrock Rovers and recorded another victory in convincing fashion – this time with Marcus Antonsson netting a brace either side of a Chris Wood penalty in a 3-0 rout.

2016/17 KIT LAUNCH

Our 2016/17 home kit was unveiled at an exclusive Elland Road event for Season Ticket Holders back in the summer, with Chris Wood, Kemar Roofe, Marcus Antonsson, Rob Green and Stuart Dallas all on hand to model Kappa's new design. The players were also joined by a selection of lucky Junior Season Ticket Holders, who proudly displayed the Greenpeace logo on their shirt, after an opening Q&A session with Garry Monk and his coaching team. Our club photographer was there to capture the action...

THE BIG
LEEDS UNITED QUIZ

Put your Leeds United knowledge to the test with our bumper quiz on all things white, yellow and blue...

1 Which player became the club's first signing of summer 2016?

2 At which two of our fellow Yorkshire clubs did United head coach Garry Monk spend time during his playing days?

3 Who was our top goalscorer for the 2015/16 season?

4 In which forthcoming year will Leeds United celebrate the club's centenary (100-year anniversary)?

5 Can you name the two Leeds United Academy graduates who were part of England's Euro 2016 squad?

6 What nationality is Garry Monk's assistant, Pep Clotet?

7 How many different goalkeepers featured in the United first team during the 2015/16 season?

8 In which year did United last win the league title?

9 Can you name the global environmental organisation whose logo features on the front of all Leeds United junior replica shirts?

10 Who progressed through the youth system to make their full United debut first, Alex Mowatt or Charlie Taylor?

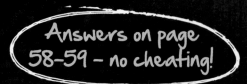

Answers on page 58–59 – no cheating!

16 Can you name our Under-23s team coach who started his playing career as a youngster at Thorp Arch?

17 Which outfield player made the most United appearances during the 2015/16 campaign?

11 Can you name the four young players who signed their first professional contracts with the club last summer?

18 At which Championship stadium did our first game of the current season take place?

12 Which team did United beat at Wembley to lift the 1972 FA Cup?

19 The club's 'Kop Cat' mascot shares his first name with which former United captain?

13 The North Stand/Kop at Elland Road is named in tribute to which legendary former United manager?

20 Can you name the twin brothers who joined the club from Doncaster Rovers in January 2016 and have played regularly for our Under-21s?

14 What would be the total if you added together the squad numbers of Chris Wood, Stuart Dallas and Toumani Diagouraga?

15 True or false? Goalkeeping coach Darryl Flahavan once had a loan spell at United during his playing days.

END OF SEASON AWARDS:

THE WINNERS

We take a look at those whose performances were rewarded with silverware at the end of the 2015/16 season…

PLAYER OF THE YEAR

CHARLIE TAYLOR

Full-back Charlie Taylor topped the official supporters' vote to claim the headline prize following a fine campaign. Taylor ended the season with 43 appearances to his name in all competitions, despite being sidelined for two months after coming down with glandular fever.

The Academy graduate's highlight came in a 2-1 victory away to MK Dons, winning the penalty for Chris Wood to open the scoring before firing home United's second goal of the afternoon and his first for the club.

"I just concentrate on my football," said Charlie. "But the awards at the end of the season are a massive bonus. You don't really think about them until they actually happen – then it's brilliant and you're absolutely buzzing about it."

YOUNG PLAYER OF THE YEAR

LEWIS COOK

For the second season running, midfielder Lewis Cook collected the club's Young Player of the Year award after another eye-catching campaign.

Cook, who was also named the Football League's Young Player of the Year, featured 47 times in all competitions during 2015/16 and scored his first senior goals along the way.

"It feels great to pick up awards at the end of the season and I was really proud to be named as the Young Player of the Year for a second year in a row," said Lewis. "It was a hard season for me but this was a good way to end it. I just need to keep on trying to improve and getting better."

PLAYER OF THE YEAR
AWARDS

LEWIS COOK vs FULHAM

Lewis Cook picked up his second trophy of last season's awards night for the stunning, long-range goal which secured a point at home to Fulham.

The England Under-19s international opened his Championship account in spectacular fashion at Elland Road, firing the ball beyond former United goalkeeper Andy Lonergan and into the top corner from around 35 yards out.

"Normally, I'd choose to pass it from there, but something just told me to shoot," Lewis explained. "I need to try it a bit more now, I think. I've been trying to shoot more and I've been practicing it in training, so I was really happy to see it fly into the top corner."

PLAYERS' PLAYER OF THE YEAR

STUART DALLAS

Northern Ireland international Stuart Dallas was voted by his teammates as the Players' Player of the Year following an impressive debut season at the club.

Dallas' 49 games in all competitions made him United's top appearance maker last term, having quickly established himself as a regular in the side after arriving from Brentford during the summer. The winger also netted five goals along the way, including a stand-out double that won the game away to Birmingham City.

"I think I made the right decision to come here," said Stuart. "It's a massive club with a massive fanbase. The fans have been brilliant with me – they support the team through thick and thin and walking out at Elland Road is just incredible."

BOBBY COLLINS UNSUNG HERO

MANDY WARD

Presented by the family of former club captain Bobby Collins, this special annual award was given to Mandy Ward of the Leeds United Ticket Office after over 31 years of continued service!

GOALS OF THE SEASON

We take a look at six of last season's finest net-busting strikes…

CHRIS WOOD
vs Derby County

DATE: Saturday August 29, 2015 **LOCATION:** iPro Stadium
FINAL SCORE: Derby County 1-2 Leeds United

The undoubted highlight of Chris Wood's debut campaign with the Whites came during the opening weeks of last season away to the division's hot promotion favourites. Having arrived from Leicester City only a couple of months earlier, the New Zealand international truly announced himself to the Leeds faithful at the iPro Stadium with a ferocious 88th-minute winner from the edge of the area, clipping the post on its way beyond former United goalkeeper Scott Carson.

"It's always nice scoring goals. But it doesn't bother me if it's 30 yards or a tap-in – a goal is a goal to me! I'll take them as they come."

"I was going to shoot but I thought I was a little bit further out... They gave me a bit more time and I just thought 'I'm going to hit it'."

ALEX MOWATT
vs Cardiff City

DATE: Tuesday November 3, 2015
LOCATION: Elland Road
FINAL SCORE: Leeds United 1-0 Cardiff City

Alex Mowatt's first goal of last season proved to be well worth the wait as his trademark long-range strike was enough for Leeds to taste victory over Cardiff City for the first time in 32 years. After being invited to stride forward, the midfielder's left-footed effort whistled into the top corner from 30 yards out, ending United's eight-month wait for three points at Elland Road and sealing a first win for then head coach Steve Evans.

ALEX MOWATT
vs Huddersfield Town

DATE: Saturday November 7, 2015
LOCATION: John Smith's Stadium
FINAL SCORE: Huddersfield Town 0-3 Leeds United

Mowatt stole the show again with another spectacular strike just four days on from his winner against Cardiff – this time in United's Yorkshire derby demolition of local rivals Huddersfield Town. Struck from a similar distance to his first of the season, the Thorp Arch graduate's unstoppable second-half thunderbolt swerved mid-air as it flew past goalkeeper Joe Murphy to wrap up a convincing victory at the John Smith's Stadium, earning Mowatt another Man of the Match award.

"I definitely preferred this one. It was a derby game and that settled it, really, the third goal. They were never coming back from 3-0 down. I was well happy with it."

LEWIS COOK
vs Fulham

DATE: Tuesday February 23, 2016
LOCATION: Elland Road
FINAL SCORE: Leeds United 1-1 Fulham

Lewis Cook's first league goal of his career – coming in his 66th Championship appearance for the club – was a worthy winner of the Goal of the Year award at the end of last season. The England Under-19s international levelled proceedings at Elland Road with a wicked, dipping strike from the best part of 35 yards out, leaving former United 'keeper Andy Lonergan helpless as he desperately flew across the Fulham goal line.

"Normally, I'd choose to pass it from there, but something just told me to shoot. I need to try it a bit more now. It flew into the top corner. I was really happy with it."

STUART DALLAS
vs Birmingham City

DATE: Tuesday April 12, 2016   **LOCATION:** St Andrew's
FINAL SCORE: Birmingham City 1-2 Leeds United

Stuart Dallas bagged an eye-catching brace in United's 2-1 victory away to Birmingham City towards the end of last season, but it was his second of the evening which became an instant Goal of the Year contender. After opening the scoring with a low strike in the first half, the Northern Ireland international doubled his tally for the night with a thunderous 20-yard volley shortly after the break, teeing himself before leaving the Blues 'keeper stranded.

"You've got to take your chances to go in behind and, fortunately, I was able to control it and hit it. Sometimes they go in, sometimes they don't."

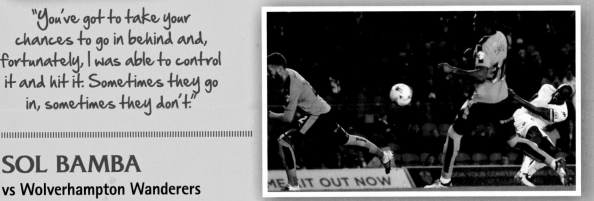

SOL BAMBA
vs Wolverhampton Wanderers

DATE: Tuesday April 19, 2016   **LOCATION:** Elland Road
FINAL SCORE: Leeds United 2-1 Wolverhampton Wanderers

Captain Sol Bamba ended last season in fine goalscoring form, including a thumping effort against Wolves which prompted the defender to admit: "I'll be lucky if I ever score a better one!" Bamba cushioned a pass from Dallas on his chest on the edge of the area, adjusted his body expertly and unleashed a sensational half-volley into the top corner to set United on their way to an impressive three points at Elland Road.

"As a defender, it's rare you find yourself in a shooting position on the edge of the box, so it was a great feeling to see it fly in."

SPOT THE DIFFERENCE

Can you spot the eight differences in this photo of Garry Monk talking tactics with Luke Murphy?

Answers on page 58-59

MEET THE SCHOLARS

These 11 young players are hoping to be stars of the future at Elland Road after signing two-year scholarship contracts with the club at the start of the season...

Alex Wollerton
(midfielder)

Alfie McCalmont
(midfielder)

Bobby Kamwa
(midfielder)

Callum Nicell

Jamie Shackleton
(midfielder)

Liam Kitching
(defender)

Matthew Keogh
(defender)

Moise Kroma
(striker)

Moses Abioye
(striker)

Robbie Gotts
(defender)

Samuel Amissah
(striker)

KEMAR ROOFE

WORDSEARCH

Can you spot the names of 10 current Leeds United players hidden within our wordsearch?

B	E	M	P	V	Z	M	G	N
E	F	Z	G	K	U	N	Y	O
R	O	N	J	R	I	W	S	S
A	O	Y	P	L	E	A	L	S
R	R	H	Y	H	C	E	F	N
D	Y	A	M	K	D	N	N	O
I	X	M	O	W	A	T	T	T
E	L	Y	O	C	H	J	R	N
C	O	O	P	E	R	H	F	A

Antonsson   Coyle   Roofe

Ayling   Green   Sacko

Berardi   Mowatt

Cooper   Murphy

Answers on page 58-59

CHRIS WOOD'S
DREAM TEAM

United striker Chris Wood becomes
the gaffer and selects his dream XI
of players he's come up against in his career...

Goalkeeper: Thibaut Courtois

"I played against him the season before last for Chelsea.
He's just quality. He's a great player already and he's
going to be a top, top 'keeper in years to come."

Formation: 4-3-3

Right Back: Thiago Silva

"I know he's a centre-back but you could imagine
him playing anywhere across the defence quite
comfortably. He's just rock solid and a real leader for
club and country."

Centre Back: Fabio Cannavaro

"I came up against him at the World Cup and he was
just unbelievable with the way he read the game and
picked balls up. He was a very good defender."

Centre Back: John Terry

"He's just solid, a proper defender. For years he's been
one of the best around and he's still right up there.
You know you're in for a battle against him."

Left Back: Marcelo

"You can see the quality he's got. I played against
him at the 2012 Olympics when he was in the same
Brazil team as Neymar. A class act."

Midfield: Steven Gerrard

"I came on at Anfield for West Brom against him nearly
six years ago. He's been a top quality player throughout
his career and he's totally unique as a midfielder."

Midfield: Andrea Pirlo

"Another one I played against at the World Cup. He's
unbelievable, his feet are a joke and his vision for a
pass is just pure quality. He's still got it."

Midfield: Cesc Fabregas

"He's pure quality and has been since he first came
through at Arsenal - he's a real technician on the
ball. He's absolutely superb and would get in most
teams."

Right Wing: Willian

"It was between him and Oscar at Chelsea, but I'll go
with Willian for the pace and quality he's got. He fits
into my 4-3-3. He had a very good season last year,
too."

Striker: Didier Drogba

"He was my idol when I was a kid and I was lucky to
play against him. He was so strong and physical, but
also a great goalscorer. He had everything you want."

Left Wing: Neymar

"I played against him at the Olympics and he was
just 'on flames' - no-one could get close to him. He
was talked about massively at the time as the next
big thing."

Courtois

Silva

Cannavaro

Terry

Marcelo

Gerrard

Pirlo

Fabregas

Willian

Drogba

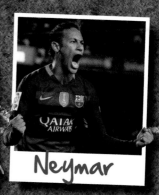

Neymar

FIRST DIVISION TITLE WINNERS,
25 YEARS ON

Take a trip down memory lane with photos from one of the club's proudest days…

2017 marks the silver anniversary of Leeds United being crowned 'The Last Champions', as Howard Wilkinson's side famously pipped bitter rivals Manchester United to the 1991/92 First Division title in the final season before the Premier League was formed.

Wilkinson remains the last English manager to lift the top-flight trophy, and what made the achievement even more remarkable was the fact that it came just two years after United had secured promotion from the Second Division.

Leeds suffered defeat just four times all season and secured the title on the penultimate day of the campaign, beating Sheffield United in a 3-2 thriller at Bramall Lane before going on to lift the trophy the following weekend at Elland Road after beating Norwich City 1-0.

Leeds United 1991/92 First Division Title-Winning Squad:

Manager: Howard Wilkinson

Goalkeepers: Mervyn Day, John Lukic, Paul Pettinger, Neil Edwards

Defenders: Tony Dorigo, Chris Fairclough, Gary Kelly, John McClelland, Jon Newsome, Mel Sterland, David Wetherall, Chris Whyte, Mike Whitlow, Dylan Kerr, Ray Wallace, Rob Bowman

Midfielders: Gordon Strachan (captain), David Batty, Gary Speed, Gary McAllister, Chris Kamara, Steve Hodge, Glynn Snodin, Simon Grayson, Scott Sellars, Mark Tinkler, Andy Williams

Forwards: Lee Chapman, Bobby Davison, Rod Wallace, Eric Cantona, Noel Whelan, Carl Shutt, Imre Varadi, Tony Agana

LIAM COOPER

leedsunited.com/superstore

CROSSWORD

Can you answer the Leeds United questions below to complete the crossword?

ACROSS

2 Who is Garry Monk's assistant at Elland Road? (3,6)

5 Chris Wood plays international football for which country? (3,7)

6 Where did United's summer 2016 pre-season tour take place? (7)

7 What was the League Cup renamed to at the start of the season? (3,3)

8 Which former England international is United's first-team coach? (5,7)

11 Our first summer signing of 2016 was born in which country? (6)

13 Which current first-team squad member has over 10 England caps to his name? (3,5)

14 Who was our second highest goalscorer last season? (5,9)

DOWN

1 From which club did Leeds sign forward Kemar Roofe? (6,6)

3 Who won the 2015/16 Player of the Year award? (7,6)

4 Can you name the young midfielder who made his senior debut on the final day of the 2015/16 season? (7,6)

9 Kyle Bartley and Matt Grimes joined on loan from which Premier League club in summer 2016? (7,4)

10 Which stand at Elland Road has two tiers? (4,5)

12 Which nationality is on-loan winger Hadi Sacko? (6)

Answers on page 58-59

ALL LEEDS AREN'T WE?
FAMOUS FANS

Celebrity Leeds fans who you may, or may not, recognise from the world of film, music and television…

Ralph Ineson

The Game of Thrones star is a lifelong United supporter and still attends as many games a season as his hectic acting schedule permits. Ralph has also featured in Harry Potter, The Office and Guardians of the Galaxy. He even had a brief role in the Damned United and his distinctive Yorkshire accent has seen him provide voiceovers for an array of television adverts.

Verne Troyer

Okay, the Hollywood actor and comedian has previously been pictured sporting an Arsenal shirt, but we'd like to think Verne is a convert to the way of the Whites after his recent visits to Elland Road. Verne, who is best known for his role as 'Mini Me' in the Austin Powers films, was in attendance for our 2-0 victory over Derby County in November 2014.

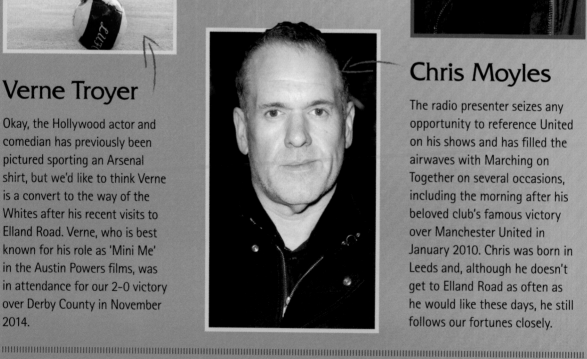

Chris Moyles

The radio presenter seizes any opportunity to reference United on his shows and has filled the airwaves with Marching on Together on several occasions, including the morning after his beloved club's famous victory over Manchester United in January 2010. Chris was born in Leeds and, although he doesn't get to Elland Road as often as he would like these days, he still follows our fortunes closely.

Other notable famous Leeds fans…

Josh Warrington (Boxer) • **Ed Miliband** (Politician) • **The Pigeon Detectives** (Band) • **Mel B** (Spice Girls)

Kaiser Chiefs

The Brit Award-winning Leeds band take their name from South African football team the Kaizer Chiefs – the former club of legendary ex-United captain Lucas Radebe. The Kaisers played a huge headline gig at Elland Road in 2008 and some of the band members can still be spotted cheering on United from the stands – home and away – providing they're not on tour.

Russell Crowe

The Gladiator star, a multi-award-winning actor, adopted Leeds as his team after watching Don Revie's great side on Match of the Day as a youngster. His brother chose Liverpool but Russell has stuck with United and was even linked with buying the club last season before ruling himself out, admitting he didn't want to spend any more time away from his children.

Kelly Jones

The Stereophonics frontman was born shortly after United won the league title in 1974 and has remained connected to the club ever since. A demanding touring calendar means Kelly is often jetting around the world, but he still keeps in touch with goings on at Elland Road. Kelly once presented good friend Wayne Rooney with a Leeds shirt with the Manchester United striker's name on the back.

Jeremy Paxman

The Leeds-born broadcaster, who hosted Newsnight on the BBC for 25 years, is a lifelong United fan and has an honorary doctorate degree from the University of Leeds. Jeremy lives in Oxfordshire now though, and is the current question master on University Challenge, meaning visits to Elland Road are difficult to squeeze in. He once interviewed fellow Leeds fan Ed Miliband in a live leadership debate.

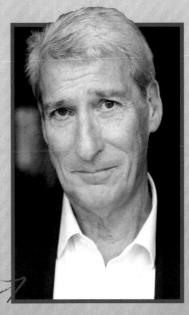

Other notable famous Leeds fans...

Chris Edwards (Kasabian Bassist) • **Jack P Shepherd** (Actor, Coronation Street) • **Colin Montgomerie** (Golfer)

MADE OF BRICKS

Elland Road, but as you've never seen it before...

In recent years, a number of intrepid football supporters have set about 'Doing the 92' – by paying a visit to every stadium in the Football League pyramid and ticking off a live match at each one on their travels.

This year, however, one nimble-fingered fan is embarking on his own unique 92-Ground Challenge... This one involves Lego bricks, and plenty of them!

As you can see from the pictures here, the early results are promising and we can hardly take our eyes off this 58x50x20cm model of Elland Road.

Creator Chris Smith told us: "I'm working on a project to build all 92 League grounds from Lego.

"There is no set order but I decided to build Elland Road to take it to the 'Yorkshire Brick Show', where it was then sold.

"It took about two weeks to build and contains over 1,500 bricks.

For more information on the pre-built Lego football stadiums, please visit **brickstand.co.uk** or email **brickstand@yahoo.co.uk.**

"I grew up in Bardsey, near Wetherby, so out of all the grounds, Elland Road is the one I've driven past the most and it was quite special to do.

"The stadiums are built by looking at lots of photos rather than going to the ground itself, as putting in too much detail wouldn't really work with the Lego.

"Out of all the grounds I have done, Elland Road was the most retweeted on Twitter, so I'd like to thank all the fans for that!"

A real work of art, we're sure you'll agree!

Follow

@LUFC
@ELLANDROAD
@LUFCTICKETS
@LUFCGRASSROOTS

LEEDS UNITED®

ANAGRAMS

Can you rearrange the anagrams below to work out the names of current Leeds United players?

1 Compare Oil

2 Doc How Sir

3 Boarding Tea Ear

4 Van Hip Kills Lip

5 Unroll Bursts

6 Fake Roomer

Answers on page 58-59

7 Darts USA Tall

8 Counts Masons Ran

QUIZ ANSWERS

Page 34-35 – The Big Leeds United Quiz

1. Which player became the club's first signing of summer 2016? **Answer: Marcus Antonsson**

2. At which two of our fellow Yorkshire clubs did United head coach Garry Monk spend time during his playing days? **Answer: Sheffield Wednesday and Barnsley**

3. Who was our top goalscorer for the 2015/16 season? **Answer: Chris Wood (13)**

4. In which forthcoming year will Leeds United celebrate the club's centenary (100-year anniversary)? **Answer: 2019**

5. Can you name the two Leeds United Academy graduates who were part of England's Euro 2016 squad? **Answer: Danny Rose and James Milner**

6. What nationality is Garry Monk's assistant, Pep Clotet? **Answer: Spanish**

7. How many different goalkeepers featured in the United first team during the 2015/16 season? **Answer: Three (Marco Silvestri, Ross Turnbull, Bailey Peacock-Farrell)**

8. In which year did United last win the league title? **Answer: 1992**

9. Can you name the global environmental organisation whose logo features on the front of all Leeds United junior replica shirts? **Answer: Greenpeace**

10. Who progressed through the youth system to make their full United debut first, Alex Mowatt or Charlie Taylor? **Answer: Charlie Taylor (2011)**

11. Can you name the four young players who signed their first professional contracts with the club last summer? **Answer: Ronaldo Vieira, Tom Pearce, Jack Vann and Michael Taylor**

12. Which team did United beat at Wembley to lift the 1972 FA Cup? **Answer: Arsenal**

13. The North Stand/Kop at Elland Road is named in tribute to which legendary former United manager? **Answer: Don Revie**

14. What would be the total if you added together the squad numbers of Chris Wood, Stuart Dallas and Toumani Diagouraga? **Answer: 28**

15. True or false? Goalkeeping coach Darryl Flahavan once had a loan spell at United during his playing days. **Answer: True (on loan from Crystal Palace in 2009)**

16. Can you name the coach of our Under-23s team who also started his playing career as a youngster at Thorp Arch? **Answer: Jason Blunt**

17. Which outfield player made the most United appearances during the 2015/16 campaign? **Answer: Stuart Dallas (49)**

18. At which Championship stadium did our first game of the current season take place? **Answer: Loftus Road**

19. The club's 'Kop Cat' mascot shares his first name with which former United captain? **Answer: Lucas Radebe**

20. Can you name the twin brothers who joined the club from Doncaster Rovers in January 2016 and have played regularly for our Under-21s? **Answer: Jack and Paul McKay**

Correct answers:

20/20: Congratulations – that's title-winning form! You're an expert on the world of Leeds United!

18-19: Well done – you're heading for promotion! There isn't much that you don't know about Leeds United!

15-17: Nice work – you've reached the play-offs! A couple of marks short of silverware, but an excellent achievement nonetheless!

10-14: Good effort – a top-half finish is something to be proud of! It's a bright start and your knowledge isn't far off the best!

5-9: Unlucky – a bottom-half finish is never the aim! Another read through the Annual is sure to see an improvement, though!

Below 5: Must try harder – you're in danger of relegation! It's time to dig deep and prove you have the knowledge!

Page 40 – Spot the Difference

1. Player's left sock has no 'LUFC' scripture

2. Manager's right leg has no badge

3. Player's armband is orange

4. Blue sock on substitutes' bench

5. Kappa logo missing from left leg of player's shorts

6. Half middle stripe on the adidas boot on substitutes' bench

7. Cone added in the bottom left

8. Player's right sock has yellow trim at the top

Page 45 – Wordsearch

B	E	M	P	V	Z	M	G	N
E	F	Z	G	K	U	N	Y	O
R	O	N	J	R	I	W	S	S
A	O	Y	P	L	E	A	L	S
R	R	H	Y	H	C	E	F	N
D	Y	A	M	K	D	N	N	O
I	X	M	O	W	A	T	T	T
E	L	Y	O	C	H	J	R	N
C	O	O	P	E	R	H	F	A

Page 57 – Anagram

1. Compare Oil = Liam Cooper

2. Doc How Sir = Chris Wood

3. Boarding Tea Ear = Gaetano Berardi

4. Van Hip Kills Lip = Kalvin Phillips

5. Unroll Bursts = Ross Turnbull

6. Fake Roomer = Kemar Roofe

7. Darts USA Tall = Stuart Dallas

8. Counts Masons Ran = Marcus Antonsson

Page 51 – Crossword

CLUB FACTS AND FIGURES

Elland Road capacity:
37,890

Elland Road pitch measurements:
115 x 74 yards

Nicknames:
'United' or 'The Whites'

First choice colours:
White with blue and gold trim

Change colours:
Yellow with blue strip

First game in Football League:
August 28 1920, Division Two v Port Vale (a)
Lost 0–2

Record attendance:
57,892 v Sunderland FA Cup 5th rnd replay
March 15 1967

Record League win:
8–0 v Leicester City, Division One, April 7 1934

Record European win:
10–0 v Lyn Oslo, European Cup 1st rnd 1st leg
September 17 1969

Record FA Cup win:
8–1 v Crystal Palace 3rd rnd January 1930

Record League Cup win:
5–1 v Mansfield Town 2nd rnd, September 1963

Record League defeat:
1–8 v Stoke City, Division One, August 27 1934

Record European defeat:
'0–4 v SK Lierse, UEFA Cup, 1st rnd, 1st leg, [day]
Sept 1971 / Barcelona, Champions League, [day]
Sept 2000

Record FA Cup defeat:
2–7 v Middlesbrough 3rd rnd, January 1946

Record League Cup defeat:
0–7 v West Ham 3rd rnd, November 1966 /
Arsenal 2nd rnd, September 1979

MATCH SEQUENCES

Unbeaten start to the season:
29 (1973/74)

Most successive wins in all competitions to start season:
8 (2009/10)

Longest undefeated run:
34 (Oct 1968 – Aug 1969)

Longest undefeated run at home:
39 (May 1968 – March 1970)

Longest undefeated run away:
17 (Oct 1968 – Aug 1969)

Successive home wins (league):
15 (Jan 2009 – Oct 2010)

Successive defeats (league):
6 (April 1947 – May 1947)

Successive games without a win (league):
17 (January 1947 – August 1947)

Longest run without a home win:
10 (February 1982 – May 1982)

Longest run without an away win:
26 (March 1939 – August 1947)

> *Leeds United came into being late in 1919 but it was 1920 when the club gained election to the Football League.*

Record League scorer in a season:
John Charles 43, Division Two 1953 – 54

Highest number of league goals in a match:
5, Gordon Hodgson v Leicester City, Division One, October 1 1938

Highest number of League goals in aggregate:
Peter Lorimer 168

Record all-time goalscorer:
Peter Lorimer 238

Record appearances in league matches:
Jack Charlton 629

Record all-time appearances:
773 Jack Charlton / Billy Bremner

Record transfer fee paid:
£18m to West Ham for Rio Ferdinand, November 2000

Record transfer fee received:
£29.1m from Manchester Utd for Rio Ferdinand, July 2002

Oldest Player:
Eddie Burbank (41yrs and 23 days) – v Hull City, April 1954

Youngest Player:
Peter Lorimer (15 years and 289 days) – v Southampton, September 1962

First schoolboy to play for club:
Tom Elliott v Norwich City, February 3, 2007

Most players used in a season:
44 (2004/05 and 2006/07)

MANAGERS

Dick Ray 1919 – 1920
Arthur Fairclough 1920 – 1927
Dick Ray 1927 – 35
Billy Hampson 1935 – 1947
Willis Edwards 1947 – 1948
Major Frank Buckley 1948 – 1953
Raich Carter 1953 – 1958
Bill Lambton 1958 – 1959
Jack Taylor 1959 – 1961
Don Revie 1961 – 1974
Brian Clough – 1974 (July-September)
Jimmy Armfield 1974 – 1978
Jock Stein 1978 (Aug – Sept)
Jimmy Adamson 1978 – 1980
Allan Clarke 1980 – 1982
Eddie Gray 1982 – 1985
Billy Bremner 1985 – 1988
Howard Wilkinson 1988 – 1996
George Graham 1996 – 1998
David O'Leary 1998 – 2002
Terry Venables 2002 – 2003
Peter Reid 2003 (Mar – Nov)
Eddie Gray 2003 – 2004
Kevin Blackwell 2004 – 2006
Dennis Wise 2006 – 2008
Gary McAllister 2008 (Jan – Dec)
Simon Grayson 2008 – 2012
Neil Warnock 2012 – 2013
Brian McDermott 2013 – 2014
David Hockaday 2014 (June – August)
Darko Milanič 2014 (September – October)
Neil Redfearn 2014 – 2015
Uwe Rosler 2015 (May – October)
Steve Evans 2015 – 2016
Garry Monk 2016 –

Can you spot our furry mascot within the crowd of Leeds United supporters at Elland Road?

Contents

Foreword

Mental Health First Aid was first developed in Canberra, Australia by Betty Kitchener and Professor Anthony Jorm at the Centre for Mental Health Research (Australian National University).

Mental Health First Aid came to Scotland in 2003 when Betty Kitchener was invited to train a small group of instructors to pilot the course across Scotland. In 2004, after a very positive response to the pilot, the course was adapted and modified for Scotland. The National Training Team for Scotland's Mental Health First Aid (SMHFA) was recruited, and in spring 2005 the first cohort of instructors in SMHFA was trained. An independent evaluation of Scotland's Mental Health First Aid reported a very positive response from both instructors and participants, leading to the development of this manual and a range of additional training materials.

Scotland's mental health FIRST AID

Using this manual

This manual has been written for people who attend the 12-hour Mental Health First Aid training course in Scotland. It is intended as a resource for use during the training course and as a reference after the course is completed.

Users may dip into specific sections for information as needed, or use it to refresh their knowledge. Readers should be aware, however, that the discussions, activities and skills covered in the 12-hour course are essential to Mental Health First Aid. The contents of this manual alone cannot cover every aspect of the training and it is only available to participants who attend a 12-hour course delivered by an approved SMHFA instructor. For quality assurance purposes and to ensure that the key messages are not taken out of context, it is not available to the general public.

Commitment to Equality
NHS Health Scotland, the writers and the developers of this material are committed to valuing diversity, and therefore promote equality within Scotland's Mental Health First Aid training. An Equality Impact Assessment was completed in 2010. Please contact NHS Health Scotland for details.

Mental illness is one of the major public health challenges in Scotland. Around one in four people are estimated to be affected by mental health problems in any given year. Improving mental health is a priority for the Scottish Government.

In addition to continuing to develop and improve access and service responses for people who experience mental illness, we want to enable people in Scotland – both individually and collectively – to be better able to help themselves in improving and sustaining their mental and physical health. With our partner agencies, we want to provide environments that are conducive to promoting health, including healthier homes, workplaces, communities and social and physical environments.

Underlying this is a need to continue to tackle Scotland's health inequalities, so that the most disadvantaged in our society can personally flourish and feel they have a stake in Scotland's future. We will not only respond to the consequences of mental health problems and poor mental wellbeing, and inequalities existing within these, but also tackle the underlying causes. As well as supporting traditional approaches to care and support, we are committed to taking action to promote mental wellbeing and reduce the prevalence of mental health problems; both approaches should, in fact, complement each other. Key aspects of mental health improvement include tackling the stigma which can be associated with mental ill health; increasing our understanding of mental illness; providing appropriate support to those experiencing mental ill health; and promoting recovery and good mental health.

The launch of Scotland's Mental Health First Aid (SMHFA) in 2004 was borne out of these imperatives. The programme, associated training and this recently updated manual have significantly contributed to an improvement in mental health – and an increase in awareness of mental health issues – in many communities over the years.

I hope that as diverse a range of people as possible will be attracted to the training programme and that they will take the opportunity to enhance their understanding of mental health issues. Improving and sustaining good mental health is important for each and every one of us, and I am confident that you will find this course both a hugely rewarding and, most importantly, enjoyable experience.

Jamie Hepburn MSP
Minister for Sport, Health Improvement and Mental Health

Scotland's mental health first aid

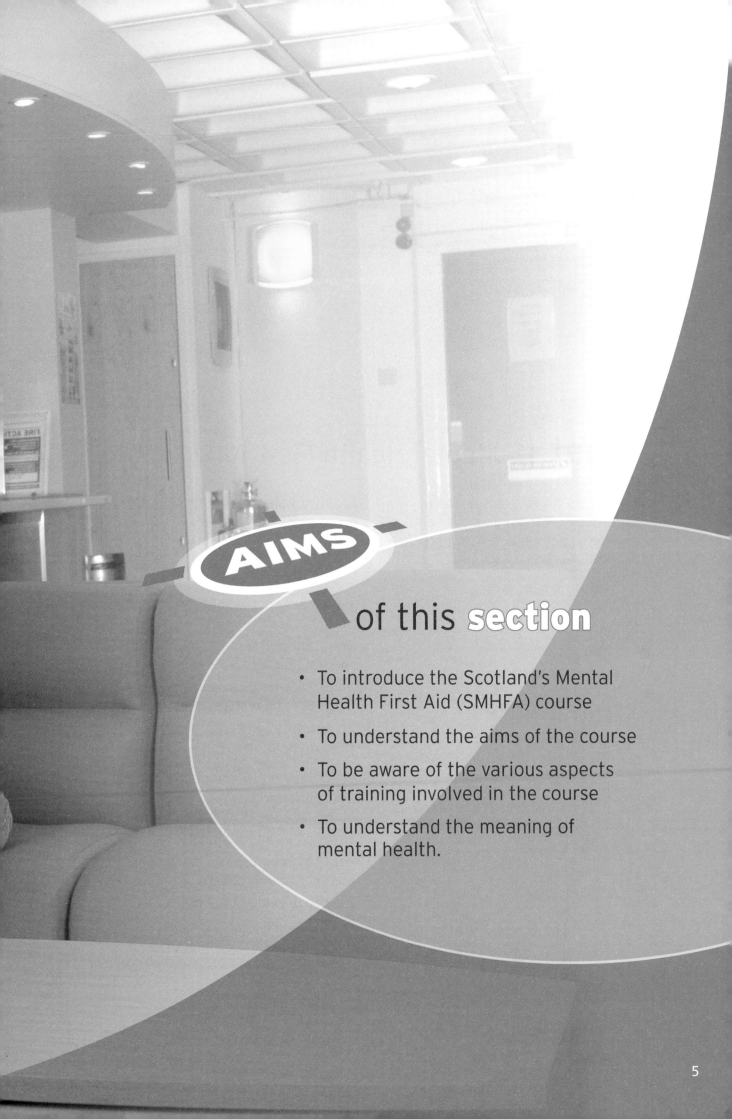

AIMS

of this **section**

- To introduce the Scotland's Mental Health First Aid (SMHFA) course

- To understand the aims of the course

- To be aware of the various aspects of training involved in the course

- To understand the meaning of mental health.

Scotland's mental health first aid

Scotland's Mental Health First Aid (SMHFA) is one of a number of projects supported by the Scottish Government to improve and promote the mental health of people in Scotland. Appendix 1: Mental Health in Scotland contains detailed information regarding the range of policies and projects that promote and support Scotland's mental health – see page 125.

What is Mental Health First Aid?

Mental Health First Aid, like any other type of first aid, is the help given to a person before appropriate professional help or treatment can be obtained.

First aid of any type has the following aims:

1. To preserve life
2. To prevent deterioration of any injury or illness
3. To promote healing
4. To provide comfort to the person who is ill, injured or distressed.

Mental Health First Aid is the help given to someone experiencing a mental health problem before other help can be accessed.

The aims of Mental Health First Aid are:

1. To preserve life
2. To provide help to prevent the mental health problem or crisis developing into a more serious state
3. To promote the recovery of good mental health
4. To provide comfort to a person experiencing distress
5. To promote understanding of mental health issues.

SMFHA does not teach people to be therapists. However, it does train people:

- How to ask about suicide
- How to recognise the signs of mental health problems or distress
- How to provide initial help
- How to guide a person towards appropriate professional help.

Why Mental Health First Aid?

There are many reasons for people to train in Mental Health First Aid.

Mental health problems are very common. As many as 1 in 4 people will experience mental health problems in any year.[1] This means that most people know someone who has personal experience of mental health problems.

Currently, 1 in 20 people have depression. Around 80% of mental health problems are anxiety and depression. GPs are likely to diagnose 60% of mental health problems, and 90% of those will be treated by their GPs. Almost 40% of absences from work are caused by mental health problems. Of all GP appointments, 70% will be patients with depression and anxiety.

Mental illness and distress has been a taboo subject in our society. This taboo is due to the stigma that surrounds mental health issues. In Western countries, people with mental health problems have been ridiculed or treated differently. For this reason, there is often a fear of speaking about such experiences.

Most people know very little about mental health. Good information and understanding about where to get effective help and treatment for mental health problems is invaluable when a crisis occurs, regardless as to the setting. Receiving help or treatment early gives people the best possible chance of recovery.

Having people in the community who are comfortable talking about mental health issues, and who offer kindness, support and appropriate information, helps to reduce distress and promote recovery.

Many people are fearful of a diagnosis of a mental health problem, believing that receiving such a diagnosis will ruin their lives. This fear may cause people to hold back from asking for help when they most need it. Fears are kept alive by ignorance and a lack of understanding. Gaining more knowledge about mental health helps to ease fears and encourage recovery.

People from other countries and cultures who live and work in Scotland, may have very different ideas about mental health, and find the Scottish health system confusing or difficult to access. For instance, Chinese medicine does not recognise the division between the mind and the body that is common in Western medicine. Therefore, a system that has separate care for mental and physical health may be difficult for a Chinese person to accept or feel confident using. Support that recognises and respects difference can help to bridge cultural differences and encourage understanding.

Professional help is not always immediately available. A 'mental health first-aider' can offer comfort and support in a crisis until help arrives.

In some instances, the person experiencing a mental health problem is not aware of the problem. Some illnesses cause the person's thinking to be affected. In other cases, the person is so distressed that they do not know how to ask for help. Others may be aware that something is wrong, but may feel afraid of judgment or rejection. A mental health first-aider is trained to approach the person, offer assistance and to listen without judgment, enabling the person to say how they feel. The first-aider can then encourage the person to get appropriate help.

Knowing how to respond in a crisis is a key part of Mental Health First Aid. It gives the first-aider confidence to know that they are offering effective help and not making things worse. SMHFA is based on a five-step action plan that can be applied in any situation in which a person is experiencing mental health problems or distress.

'It wasn't until a friend shared her knowledge from her training as a mental health first aid instructor that I realised that it would take more than doctors' appointments and medication to help make me better. In fact, I had convinced myself that I would be living with depression for the rest of my life. My friend showed me otherwise. I know now that I can help myself with the right support to take more positive steps to recover.'

(Linda Goslan, BBC Scotland, June 2005.)

Using the Skills of Mental Health First Aid

Sometimes people are worried that being trained as a mental health first-aider will mean that they have to take responsibility for others even when this is too emotionally demanding or time consuming. This is an understandable concern, but it is based on a misconception. People trained in mental health first aid are ordinary people who have been trained in what to do during a mental health crisis. However, their role is only essential in the very short term, until other help can be found. That other help can come in a variety of forms – from the person's family or friends, a GP, a telephone helpline, a hospital Accident and Emergency department, or an ambulance.

A key thing to remember is that although the first-aider has been trained how to respond, they are never obliged to intervene.

Keeping **safe**

The mental health first-aider must always put his or her own wellbeing and safety first. Taking care of one's own health and safety can mean a variety of things depending on the situation.

- Occasionally, people in a distressed state can become threatening to others due to fear or confusion. If you are in any doubt about your own or others' safety, move away from the person and call for urgent help.

- Even when the person appears threatening or unsafe, it is best to remain calm and continue to reassure the person of your concern for their wellbeing.

- Be honest with the person. Tell them that you are concerned and are calling for help.

- Sometimes people who are distressed become very attached to those who offer them help or comfort. As a first-aider, you are not obliged to take responsibility for the person's long-term wellbeing and you should not agree to do more than you feel is reasonable. Your decision may depend on your relationship with the person and your own personal situation, but remember that the person's wellbeing is not solely in your hands. A first-aider gives initial help before other help is available.

- Helping a distressed person is stressful and sometimes very upsetting. A first-aider needs to practise good self-care.

- Remember we are human beings and we cannot fix everything. When things do not go well with a person we are trying to help, it is important that we do not give ourselves a hard time.

First Aid for **Mental Health**

Ask about suicide

Listen non-judgmentally

Give reassurance and information

Encourage the person to get appropriate help

Encourage self-help strategies

Mental Health First Aid is the first step in helping a person experiencing a mental health crisis, and is intended to be used until other help arrives.

Just like physical first aid, the first aim of mental health first aid is to preserve life.

Evidence shows that many people experiencing a mental health crisis have thoughts of suicide, and some people act on these thoughts. This is why asking about suicide is the first step in offering help.

step 1

Ask about suicide

This does not mean that you should ask everyone you meet about suicide, regardless of their situation. What it does mean is that when you suspect that a person may be having suicidal thoughts, because of their level of pain or distress, or because of their situation, or even because you have a gut feeling that they may be considering suicide, you should ask them.

This may seem very challenging and difficult to begin with, but the SMHFA course covers the skills and practice that will make this step feel more natural.

Once we are sure that the person is not in immediate danger we can put the next step into practice.

Listen non-judgmentally

People who are feeling distressed or experiencing mental health problems can feel that no one is able to listen to them, or to accept their feelings without judging them as weak or inferior. Being able to listen to the person, and offering them the simple human kindness of the time to talk about how they feel, can help them realise that they are not alone.

Give reassurance and information

This is not about offering advice or solving the person's problems. It is about reassuring them that there is effective help available and that there are things we can do immediately to help the situation.

Encourage the person to get professional help

This is essential to their recovery. Help may be in the form of their GP, other support groups or therapy. The help they need will depend on the type of problems they are experiencing. This course will provide you with information on where different types of help can be found quickly.

Encourage self-help strategies

When a person is experiencing mental health problems, there are things that can be done in the short term to alleviate their distress. Similarly, when treatment is underway there are often things that a person can do to help recovery.

All of these steps are covered in detail in the course and in this manual.

What is **mental health?**

The World Health Organisation defines health as:

> '...a state of (complete) physical, mental and social
> wellbeing and not merely the absence of disease or infirmity.'

Health is a positive concept that relates to every part of our lives. We cannot easily separate our physical and mental health, both of which can be influenced by other factors in our lives.

The term 'mental health' is often misunderstood. When asked about mental health people often assume it to be a negative term that means mental illness.

> 'Mental health means our ability to enjoy life and cope
> with its challenges. In a nutshell, are we able to get on and do
> the things we want to do? It's not a by-word for 'mental illness'.
> A mental illness is a problem that affects mental health
> (just like a broken leg affects physical health).' [2]

Just as physical health refers to everything related to the health of our bodies, mental health refers to the health of our minds and emotions. Mental health influences how we think and feel about ourselves and about others, as well as how we respond to things that happen to us. It affects our work, learning, relationships, and the way we cope with ordinary life events such as moving house, having children or experiencing bereavement.

Mental health is about everyone. Our physical health changes over time and so does our mental health. Some days we feel better than other days, and at some times in our lives, we experience more stress and distress than in others. Some of life's most challenging events cause us to experience poor mental health, but over time we recover. All of this is normal, and all of it is about our mental health.

> 'Everyone has mental health needs, whether or not they have
> a diagnosis. These needs are met, or not met, at home, in families,
> at work, on the streets, in schools and neighbourhoods, in prisons
> and hospitals, where people feel respected, included and safe,
> or on the margins, in fear and excluded.' [3]

Sometimes people develop more severe mental health problems that need professional treatment. When this happens, it is a good idea to remember that the same thing happens in physical health. At times, we develop an illness that requires medical or other treatment. In some cases, there are things we can do to protect ourselves from getting a physical or mental illness.

It can also happen for no obvious reason. Any one of us could become unwell in our lifetimes. In this manual, you will find information about how people can care for their own mental health as well as how to respond if a person becomes very distressed or unwell.

If a person appears to be experiencing a mental health problem and is distressed, it is important to get help as quickly as possible. Left untreated, some mental health problems will get worse, causing major changes to a person's thinking, emotions and behaviour. These changes can seriously disrupt the person's work, home and social life.

'Mental health is sometimes described as underpinning all health and wellbeing, because of growing research evidence of the impact of how people think and feel on their physical health.' [4]

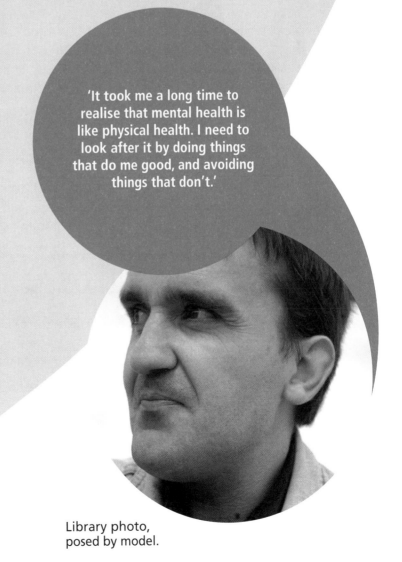

'It took me a long time to realise that mental health is like physical health. I need to look after it by doing things that do me good, and avoiding things that don't.'

Library photo, posed by model.

13

Attitudes to mental health issues

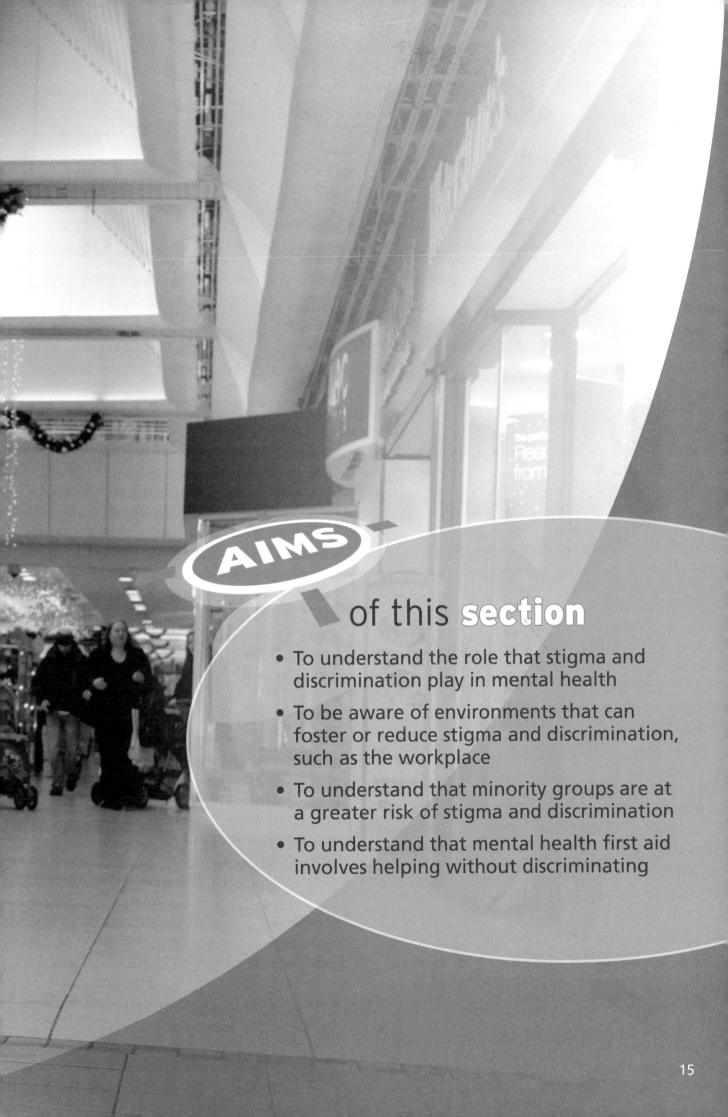

AIMS

of this **section**

- To understand the role that stigma and discrimination play in mental health

- To be aware of environments that can foster or reduce stigma and discrimination, such as the workplace

- To understand that minority groups are at a greater risk of stigma and discrimination

- To understand that mental health first aid involves helping without discriminating

'Some colleagues avoided me and dropped their eyes rather than greet me. Others began to patronise me even though they had always given me professional respect. People talked about me as though I wasn't there or fell out with me for no reason. I left the post a few months later.' [5]

Library photo,
posed by model.

Stigma and Myth

Most people know that it is not appropriate to deliberately treat someone with mental health problems badly. This awareness means that stigma is often expressed in less obvious ways, such as unkind jokes or ignoring a person. Stigma and the fear of stigma is a serious issue that has an effect on people's ability to cope with and recover from a mental health problem.

There is a lot of evidence to show that people are treated differently when they experience a mental health problem.

Stigma is based on myths and false assumptions about mental health problems. Therefore, it is best addressed by gaining knowledge and an understanding of the facts.

Some important facts
about mental health problems

- Mental health problems are common and can affect anyone.

- People with mental health problems do not lose their personality or intelligence, although the symptoms can sometimes change the way a person behaves when they are unwell.

- People with mental health problems usually recover – there is a better chance of recovery from mental health problems than from some physical illnesses.

- People with mental health problems want to work and to contribute to society, but it is often other people's attitudes that prevent them doing so.

- Two thirds of employers, when asked, said that they did not feel comfortable employing a person with a mental health problem.

- Many people with mental health problems continue to live life to the full, working and enjoying positive relationships and activities.

16

Recent research has found that attitudes towards people with mental health have improved significantly in Scotland since anti-stigma campaigns like 'see me' were introduced. We can make a difference to people's mental health by gaining understanding and knowledge, and sharing it with others. We can also make a difference by treating people with mental health problems as equals, and offering kindness and support when they are unwell.[6]

Models of Mental Health

There are many different ways of explaining mental health issues. Different models emphasise different aspects of mental health, such as the impact society and culture have on a person's mental health. Other models of mental health are briefly described in Appendix 2: Other Models of Health, on page 127.

For the purposes of this course, we have selected the Mental Health Continuum as a useful model to show that mental health changes over time and that mental health issues are about everyone.

- Sometimes, having a severe and enduring mental illness has a devastating effect on people's lives. With the right treatment and support, the person has a better chance of improvement and recovery.

- People with schizophrenia do not have a split personality.

- People with severe and enduring mental health problems are not usually dangerous - in fact, they are more likely to be victims of crimes.

- People with mental health problems are not weak and they do not bring the problems on themselves.

- A growing body of evidence suggests that mental health problems cannot be separated from physical health, as the mind and body are closely interrelated.

- Sometimes people dismiss other's mental health problems or distress by judging them as weak. This is no more helpful or appropriate than judging someone for having a physical illness or disability.

- Ordinary members of the public can help people experiencing mental health problems and make a real difference to their recovery.

The Mental Health
Continuum

Mental health and illness has sometimes been described as a spectrum. People at one end of the line or spectrum are very well, and those at the other end are very unwell with a serious mental illness. In the middle might be people who have minor mental health problems.

'On two occasions I lied when I applied for jobs. I said that my two-year absence from employment was due to a term spent in prison. I was accepted for the first and shortlisted for the second. Whenever I've been truthful about my psychiatric past, I have never been accepted for a job.' [7]

This idea is not a very helpful method to understand mental health. It can lead us to make some false assumptions. For example, one may falsely assume that most people are 'well' and that a few people, who are a long way removed at the other end of the spectrum, are 'ill' or 'mad'. This assumption creates a distance between people and causes fear. Another assumption is that once you know your place on the spectrum, it is where you will stay unless something dramatic happens to change it. This denies the fact that we can make a big difference to our own mental health, both positively and negatively. It also does not take account of the fact that our mental health changes a lot over relatively short periods of time.

Library photo, posed by model

A different and more helpful way of thinking about mental health is the continuum:

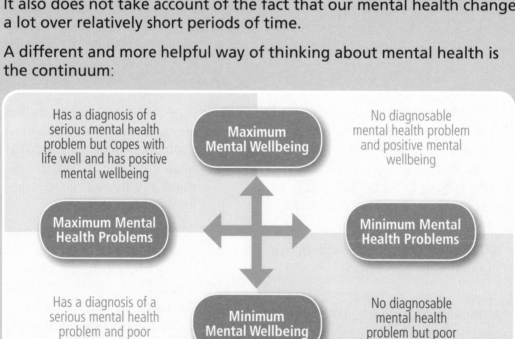

Has a diagnosis of a serious mental health problem but copes with life well and has positive mental wellbeing	**Maximum Mental Wellbeing**	No diagnosable mental health problem and positive mental wellbeing
Maximum Mental Health Problems		**Minimum Mental Health Problems**
Has a diagnosis of a serious mental health problem and poor mental wellbeing	**Minimum Mental Wellbeing**	No diagnosable mental health problem but poor mental wellbeing

Adapted from Tudor K. *Mental Health Promotion: Paradigms and Practice*. 1996.

The four quadrants of the Mental Health Continuum represent different possible times and situations in a person's life.

On the right-hand side of the diagram, two possible situations are described.

Even if a person has no diagnosable illness, they can have either positive or negative mental wellbeing. Usually the person's mental health will be affected by life events. If faced with redundancy or the break up of a long-term relationship, the person may find themselves at the lower end of the continuum, experiencing poor mental wellbeing. If things are going well and the person is looking after their emotional, mental and physical health they may be higher up the continuum.

Similarly, on the left hand side of the diagram we see that a person with a diagnosed illness can also be experiencing either positive or negative mental wellbeing.

With the right treatment and proper supports in place, the person can live a happy and fulfilled life whether or not they are experiencing symptoms. Living life to the full may involve having meaningful things to do, having good relationships, a satisfying social life and good self-esteem. On the other hand, without the right treatment and support the person may experience negative mental health.

Being at the lower end of the Mental Health Continuum puts people at greater risk of suicide, whether they have a mental illness or not.

Given that 1 in 4 Scottish adults will experience mental health problems at some time in their lives, we can see that it is possible for us to move into all four corners of the continuum at different times.

Knowing that mental health changes over time can help us to look after our own wellbeing. It can also help us to be more understanding and supportive of others when they are experiencing poor mental health.

Some common myths about mental health problems

Myth:
Only a few people get mental illnesses and they are unusual or odd, so it is obvious who they are.

Fact:
Mental health problems are common and we are often unaware of the person's diagnosis.

Myth:
People with a diagnosis of mental illness are going to struggle for the rest of their lives.

Fact:
Most people recover from mental illness and go on to live fulfilling lives. Recovery is a unique and personal journey and often the person feels that they experienced personal growth and a new way of being through the process of recovery.

Myth:
People who attempt suicide or self-harm are doing it to get attention and are not really serious.

Fact:
All suicidal thoughts and self-harm, as well as all other forms and expressions of distress are serious. Dismissing another person's feelings as attention seeking only makes them withdraw from asking for help and may result in death or serious injury.

Myth:
People who have mental illnesses have brought it upon themselves, or their parents are to blame.

Fact:
Anyone can experience mental illness or experience mental distress regardless of their background or upbringing. Some people are more at risk through circumstances beyond their own control.

Understanding
the Mental Health Continuum

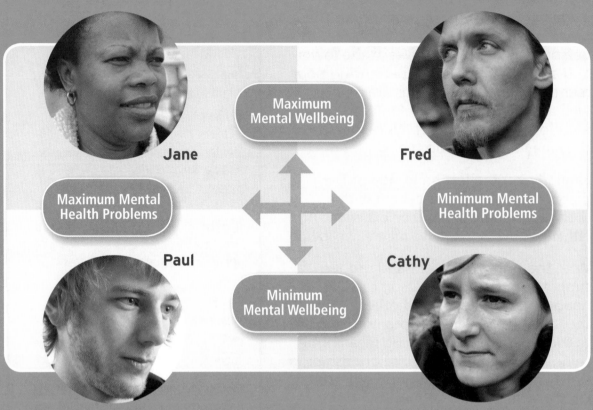

Adapted from Tudor K. *Mental Health Promotion: Paradigms and Practice*. 1996.

Each of the four people in the diagram above is in a different part of the continuum. Read on to find out more about them.

It is a wet Monday morning:

Cathy feels awful. All weekend she has been arguing with her partner. Things had been going badly for several months but this weekend everything came to a head. Finally, last night her partner told her that he was leaving because he couldn't bear to live with her nagging any more. She suspects that he has another woman but he denies it. Last night she couldn't sleep because she felt so alone and rejected. She is worried about money and wonders how she will tell her friends and family what has happened. Cathy's mental wellbeing is very low today although she has no mental illness.

Paul got a diagnosis of major depression ten years ago. Sometimes the symptoms go away for a time but so far they have always returned. Today Paul is having a bad day. He feels frightened because he feels so depressed he has been having thoughts of suicide. He got very drunk on Friday night and made a lot of noise and the neighbours have complained. He has tried to call his community psychiatric nurse but he only got the answering machine. He couldn't find the words to leave a message. He has nowhere to go and can't think how to get help. Paul has a mental illness and today his mental wellbeing is poor.

Jane was diagnosed with schizophrenia five years ago. Many of the symptoms go away for periods of time but she often hears voices. Jane has learned to live with her voices and she knows how to tell them to be quiet when she needs to concentrate on other things. Jane went to Art College and she has a job at the local council in the publishing department. She loves her work and today she is helping prepare some new leaflets on equality. Her boss has particularly asked for her input on the leaflet because he knows that she has personal experience. Jane understands that recovery means different things to different people and she has found ways to keep herself well using a range of different support and medication. Jane has a diagnosis of a serious mental illness and today her mental wellbeing is very good.

Fred is having a great day. He and his partner Michael have been talking all weekend about arranging their civil partnership. For many years, Fred found it difficult to accept his sexuality but now he feels confident and realises that accepting himself is important for his self-esteem. Fred has worked hard at understanding what positive mental health means for him and therefore is careful about how much he drinks and he takes regular exercise. Today Fred has no diagnosis of a mental health problem and his mental wellbeing is good.

All the four people above have been in different places on the continuum at different times in their lives. We can move around in the continuum for many reasons. Our mental wellbeing can be affected by circumstances outside our control, as well as by the way we look after ourselves. When things that we cannot control have a negative effect on our mental wellbeing, we can do something positive by taking good care of ourselves.

Read the Recovery section on page 26 for more information about what helps when our mental health is not good.

'When I was diagnosed with depression everyone at school thought it was an attention thing. Everything became so much harder and I was having panic attacks in classes which made them think I was seeking attention more, which made things worse still!' [8]

Library photo, posed by model.

Society, Culture and Diversity

Current thinking on mental health suggests that it is best to consider the whole person – rather than try to separate mental health from other areas of life. Each of us is a complex blend of physical, emotional, social, cultural and spiritual factors.

The way we cope with life and respond to life events is affected by our experiences, and individual characteristics such as personality. This means that there is no such thing as equality where mental health is concerned. Some people are disadvantaged by emotional or social deprivation. Others are disadvantaged by the fact that they are perceived as being different, and they experience discrimination as a result. Some people appear to have greater risk of developing mental health problems or a serious mental illness for no obvious reason.

There is a lot of evidence to suggest that social and economic deprivation makes a person more susceptible to all kinds of ill health, including mental ill health.

Mental health problems are more common in socially disadvantaged populations and in areas of deprivation. They are associated with unemployment, low education levels, low income and a poor standard of living.[9] This same underprivileged population experiences the highest prevalence of anxiety and depression.[10]

There is strong evidence of a connection between poverty, unemployment, social isolation and schizophrenia.[11] Deprivation is also associated with a number of negative experiences, such as having symptoms for longer, experiencing more frequent episodes of illness, having a poorer quality of care, and having a lower chance of recovery.[12]

Working **with diversity**

People trained in Mental Health First Aid are not expected to have specialist knowledge of different groups' attitudes and beliefs about mental health. The most important thing is to avoid making assumptions about the person to whom you are offering support. For instance, do not assume that the person shares the same attitudes as you hold. When suggesting that a person seeks further help, it is best to ask who they would feel most comfortable approaching rather than immediately suggesting the GP. Similarly, it is best to use simple language like 'low mood' or 'sadness' rather than using terms like depression when talking about a person's mood or feelings.

These guidelines hold true in any situation. It is always better to avoid making assumptions about another person and to check out that person's feelings and preferences before offering advice and support.

In Scotland, we need to pay proper attention to positive mental health and wellbeing. We can do this by promoting positive mental health, providing support so that the quality of life is improved, acting against social exclusion, and promoting the rights of people by addressing inequalities in mental health.[13]

Being perceived as different to the majority of people around you has an impact on mental health. This means that people with physical disabilities, gay, lesbian, bisexual or transgendered people, people with learning difficulties and people from black and minority ethnic groups are all more likely to experience mental health problems.

There is substantial literature regarding the impact on health of all forms of discrimination, whether on the grounds of race and ethnicity, age, gender, religion or sexual orientation. It adversely impacts mental health, affecting a person's dignity and self-esteem. It can lead to a sense of alienation, isolation, fear, and intimidation. It can make it difficult for individuals to feel socially included and to integrate into society.[14]

Difference is a problem not because of the perceived difference itself, but because of the attitude of the majority of the population towards people who appear different. We live in a culture that encourages similarity. We notice when people dress differently, live differently or act differently. Western culture has been slow to recognise how badly people are affected by being treated less favourably because of perceived difference.

The law now protects certain people and groups from discrimination and disadvantage. However, in order to foster positive mental health in society, we all need to think about our attitudes and find ways to treat one another with equal respect and care.

Mental Health First Aid training can make an enormous difference to the mental health of society because it models good practice, by offering kindness and support to people in mental distress – regardless of their ethnic heritage, sexuality, religion, economic status, health, ability, age or gender.

See Appendix 3: Inequality and Mental Health, on page 129 for more information.

Recovery

AIMS

of this section

- To understand that recovery is both possible and likely

- To understand that recovery is an individual process

- To know how to help support a person to recover.

Recovery from Mental Health Problems

> 'Two to three years ago I realised that you really could
> recover... I thought once you had it that was it – it was stuck.
> But you can recover.' [15]

For some people mental health problems may be a 'one off', causing distress for a relatively short period in a person's life. For others, mental health problems may be longer term, possibly returning at different times or causing long-term challenges. However, one thing is clear, people can and do recover from mental health problems – no matter how serious or long-term they are.

Recovery is a deeply personal and individual process. For some, it means getting back to 'normal' or back to the way things were before a period of illness. Others consider it to mean not experiencing symptoms of the illness anymore. People who have had long-term problems often describe a process of growth and development, in the presence or absence of symptoms. Many people describe it as a journey in which they become active in managing and controlling their own wellbeing and recovery.

Recovery is a key message in Scotland's Mental Health First Aid. The presence of hope and the expectation of recovery is one of the most important forms of support we can give a person with a mental health problem.

The things that help everyone recover from physical illness or painful life events are the same things that help people recover from mental illness.

The Scottish Recovery Network has been working since 2004 to:

- Raise awareness of recovery
- Develop a better understanding of the factors which help and hinder recovery
- Build capacity for recovery by sharing information and supporting efforts to promote recovery.

A major part of the initial work of the network involved a large scale Narrative Research Project. As part of this project, 64 people from Scotland, who described themselves as in recovery, or having recovered from a long-term mental health problem, were interviewed.

Try this...

Write down as many things as you can think of that have helped you recover from a difficult experience or an illness. Look at your list. Most of the things you have included will be true for the majority of people recovering from a mental health problem.

Key findings from that research included:

- The importance of having a positive identity focused on wellness, strengths and recovery.

- The need to be involved in activities which provide meaning and purpose, and to pace and control that involvement. Such activities included volunteering, paid employment and creativity.

- The importance of relationships based on hope, belief and trust.

- The need for easy access to services and treatments that are focused on recovery.

'Recovery is being able to live a meaningful and satisfying life, as defined by each person, in the presence or absence of symptoms. It is about having control over your own life. Each individual's recovery, like his or her experience of the mental health problems or illness, is a unique and deeply personal process.' [15]

Many people described the importance of believing in the possibility of recovery. They described how taking a more optimistic approach to their illness created hope, a feeling of self-worth and confidence. It helped them create a new identity as a person who was in recovery.

Library photo, posed by model.

It is rare for anyone to return to the way they were before a major life event. Our experiences change us, and it is often true that people who have experienced serious and distressing life events say that in the longer term they have grown and developed through them. This is part of the recovery message. People who have had a diagnosis of serious mental health problems often report that embarking on the journey of recovery and finding ways to live fulfilling lives has enabled them to grow. They have discovered a part of themselves they could not have known otherwise. Another similarly strong theme was focused around being in control and making choices.

Learning about recovery helps a mental health first-aider recognise the importance of relating to a person who is in distress or unwell as more than just an immediate crisis to be dealt with. We can help the process of recovery by speaking to the person with respect rather than talking down to them, and also to speak with hope and reassurance.

Learning about recovery can also help protect us from becoming unwell. Understanding what helps us recover is a good basis for helping our own and others' mental health.

'I think the thing that prevented recovery was that I didn't know anything else. I'd got a mental illness. There's some safety in being ill. Although I hated every minute of it, there was still some security in that.' [15]

Library photo, posed by model.

Recovery-focused Services

Learning directly from people's experience of recovery can offer new and different approaches to the way mental health services are offered. This is sometimes referred to as developing 'recovery-focused' or 'recovery-oriented' services. There are many initiatives in Scotland, and around the world, which are designed to ensure that services are developed incorporating the principles of recovery. Scottish initiatives include work to introduce recovery indicators and to promote self-management tools, such as Wellness Recovery Action Planning and the introduction of new training for the mental health workforce.

Organisations

Scottish Recovery Network
www.scottishrecovery.net
Tel: 0141 240 7790
Email: info@scottishrecovery.net

Promotes and supports recovery from long-term mental health problems in Scotland and Wellness Recovery Action Planning (WRAP). Also provides a range of printed resources to support your training.
Spirituality is different for everyone. Here are some helpful resources:

Royal College of Psychiatrists
Spirituality and Mental Health (2006).
www.rcpsych.ac.uk/mentalhealthinfo/treatments/spiritualityandmentalhealth.aspx

Rethink
Spirituality, Religion and Mental Illness Factsheet (2015).
www.rethink.org/resources/s

NES – Spirituality Care Matters publication
www.nes.scot.nhs.uk/education-and-training/by-discipline/spiritual-care/about-spiritual-care/publications/spiritual-care-matters-an-introductory-resource-for-all-nhs-scotland-staff.aspx

Alcohol and drugs

AIMS of this **section**

- To understand the relationship between alcohol, drugs and mental health

- To understand self-medication

- To understand the effects of alcohol and drugs on mental health.

Alcohol and Drugs

Alcohol is the social drug of choice for many people in Scotland. As a nation we celebrate births, marriages, birthdays, new jobs, retirement and the end of the working week with alcohol. It is present at every important life event and used to comfort the bereaved at deaths and funerals. Colleagues and friends can discuss excessive drinking habits with pride rather than embarrassment because alcohol is so much a feature of Scottish social life. Some people report that it is difficult to be a non-drinker in Scotland, as alcohol is pressed upon them in an attempt to draw them into the social circle.

Safe drinking is integral to good mental health, as is the need to understand the nature and effects of alcohol and drugs on mental health.

When we are suffering from a physical problem such as a severe headache or toothache, it is natural to reach for medication to take the pain away. Similarly, using alcohol and drugs when we are experiencing mental distress is often seen as a way of taking mental pain away. For a short time, we may feel better because there is a barrier between ourselves and the pain. Sometimes we drink so heavily that we cannot feel anything at all, and in acute mental distress, this might seem to be the ideal answer. Unfortunately using alcohol and drugs to take mental pain away does not have the long-term benefit we might hope for.

For the purposes of this course, we have put drugs into the categories of Stimulants, Depressants and Hallucinogens. Alcohol is included as a depressant drug. Some drugs have a combination of effects.

Key facts
about alcohol and drugs

- Dependency on alcohol is one of the most common mental health problems in Scotland.

- Alcohol and drugs are often used as self-medication for mental pain or distress.

- In most cases, alcohol and drugs make symptoms worse, not better.

- 65% of suicides involve alcohol.

- Caffeine, which is found in coffee, tea, chocolate and many soft drinks, makes anxiety worse.

- For some people, the use of recreational drugs is associated with the first episode of a serious mental health problem.

Stimulant drugs stimulate the brain and the central nervous system of the body, generally making the user more awake and more energetic. Stimulants tend to carry particular risks to the cardiovascular system, making users more prone to heart attacks or strokes.

Depressant drugs are the opposite of stimulants – they suppress brain activity and the central nervous system, generally making the user calmer and sleepier. In high doses, depressants can cause the system to be suppressed so much that the user stops breathing, which can be fatal.

Hallucinogenic drugs do not necessarily stimulate or depress the brain, but change how the user perceives sounds, colours and the world around them. The user can see, hear and imagine things that are not real (hallucinate).

Stimulants, hallucinogens and depressants can all have a negative impact on a person's mental health. Once the initial effect of a drug has gone, the person can be left feeling worse than ever – both physically and mentally (hangover or 'come down').

For some people, this further episode of pain leads them to consume even more, and to do so ever more frequently in an attempt to avoid a return to painful reality. Before long, the person may have entered a cycle of substance misuse that becomes a habit – making work, relationships and responsibilities hard to keep up. This cycle of self-medication and avoidance of mental distress can potentially lead to loss of security, home and employment thereby making any existing mental health problems far worse.

Using alcohol as self-medication or as a way to cope with life's problems is common across the general population, as well as in those with a diagnosis of a mental health problem.

'I was a carer for my mother and an elderly relative. I found I was not able to deal with all the emotions and drank to help me block the emotions out, not to feel anxious, not to have a million different worries going around my head. It's partly to do with the way I learnt to deal with things. I drank to medicate myself.' [16]

Library photo, posed by model.

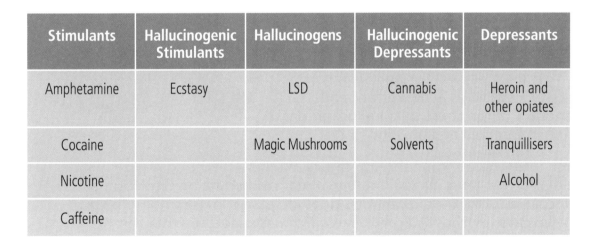

Stimulants	Hallucinogenic Stimulants	Hallucinogens	Hallucinogenic Depressants	Depressants
Amphetamine	Ecstasy	LSD	Cannabis	Heroin and other opiates
Cocaine		Magic Mushrooms	Solvents	Tranquillisers
Nicotine				Alcohol
Caffeine				

Alcohol
and Mental Health

Alcohol affects the parts of the brain that deal with stress, anxiety and depression. It eases social anxiety by reducing inhibitions, so that the person feels more relaxed in a social setting. Conversation flows more freely and the person feels more confident. Unfortunately, alcohol also limits the natural release of chemicals that normally ease feelings of anxiety and depression, so the person feels worse once the effects have worn off. Alcohol features in many suicides and accidental deaths because it reduces the inhibitions that normally help us to keep ourselves safe.

This reduction of inhibitions can also cause the person's real feelings to emerge. The normal ability to keep emotions in balance and under control is reduced, and the person can begin to experience these emotions to the full. This could explain why some people become angry, aggressive or emotional when drinking – the normal social controls are gone and their feelings are free to emerge.

About 40% of people with a diagnosis of schizophrenia report heavy usage of alcohol and drugs. 'Dual diagnosis' is the term used when a person has both a severe mental illness and a problem with alcohol.

Cannabis
and Mental Health

Cannabis is the most widely used illegal drug in the UK. Classified as a 'depressant and hallucinogen', it can cause mild hallucinations, and trigger paranoia and anxiety.

Research into whether cannabis use causes mental ill health is contentious. In 2007, research reported in the medical journal *The Lancet* found that using cannabis does increase the risk of developing mental illnesses (psychosis). Previous research has suggested that the onset of mental illness only occurs when a person is already vulnerable. The 2008 report on cannabis from the Advisory Council on the Misuse of Drugs concluded that the evidence points to a probable, but weak, causal link between psychosis and cannabis use. The Council was unconvinced that there is a causal relationship between the use of cannabis and the development of anxiety and depression.[17]

Stimulants
and Mental Health

Amphetamines (speed, whiz, billy), cocaine (coke, charlie) and caffeine are all stimulant drugs. Their effect is to give the user a burst of energy over a number of hours.

The after-effects of taking amphetamines and cocaine are extremely unpleasant and the user will often take more of the substance to try to feel better.

The more a person uses stimulants, the more they need to take because the effects get less as the body becomes accustomed to them. The feelings of low mood and mental distress when coming down from the drug are very unpleasant and may make mental health problems worse. Users are often left feeling paranoid, agitated, very low in spirit and unable to sleep. While the uplifting effects of taking stimulants may provide temporary relief from depressive or other symptoms of mental illness, the after-effects can leave the person feeling much worse.[18]

Caffeine, though legal, can contribute to anxious states and disrupt sleep. It should be used in moderation.

Ecstasy (MDMA, eccies, E) is a stimulant with some hallucinogenic effects. It operates by causing the release of serotonin in the brain. Serotonin is a mood-regulating chemical found in the brain.

The 'high' that users of ecstasy experience involves:

- Ecstatic moods (hence the name)
- Heightened senses
- Powerful feelings of wellbeing
- Strong feelings of empathy with others.

The 'low' or 'come-down' from ecstasy involves:

- Immediately afterwards, users may be unable to sleep properly
- For two to three days after using it, users report feeling very down or low.

Ecstasy usually comes in pill form, and is often mixed with amphetamines and other illegal drugs. These have added dangers for people with mental health problems.

People trained in Mental Health First Aid are encouraged not to make judgments about other people's lifestyles. However, knowledge of the risks of certain lifestyle choices can help people make informed decisions.

Important facts
about alcohol and mental health [16]

- Alcohol use can lead to symptoms of mental health problems. Some people experience this with only a small amount of alcohol.

- Becoming dependent on alcohol to cope with life can lead to psychological problems.

- Getting drunk can lead to risky or embarrassing behaviour that leads to longer term problems.

- Heavy drinkers who stop drinking without properly trained support can experience psychiatric symptoms.

- Alcohol can make an existing mental health problem worse.

- Alcohol interferes with medication and can cause it to not work properly.

- As with all drugs, the body becomes accustomed to alcohol so that a person needs to drink more to get the same effect.

Organisations

Know the Score
www.knowthescore.info
Tel: 0800 587 5879

A free and confidential drugs information and advice line.

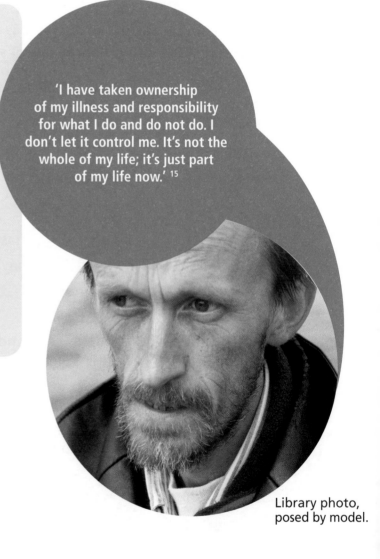

'I have taken ownership of my illness and responsibility for what I do and do not do. I don't let it control me. It's not the whole of my life; it's just part of my life now.' [15]

Library photo, posed by model.

Suicide

AIMS

of this **section**

- To understand why and how we should talk about suicide
- To be aware of suicide statistics in Scotland
- To be aware of suicide related organisations and support services
- To be able to apply ALGEE when a person appears to be at risk of suicide
- To be aware of further training courses specialising in suicide intervention.

The material in this section has been adapted from suicideTALK, with the kind permission of LivingWorks. For more training information, visit www.chooselife.net

'Most people contemplating suicide do not want to die. They just want to stop the pain and difficulties they are experiencing.'

(Choose Life – A National Strategy and Action Plan to Prevent Suicide in Scotland 2003–13.)

Should We Talk About Suicide?

Generally, people avoid talking openly about suicide. This may be because historically suicide was thought of as wrong, evil, sinful or illegal and it therefore became a taboo subject. We may not be aware of these strong cultural messages, and we may not be aware that we are avoiding talking about suicide.

Some people assume that the purpose of these underlying cultural messages is to help prevent or reduce suicide. They think that if we do not talk about suicide and it is obviously considered a taboo subject, then people will be discouraged from considering suicide. It is now clear, after centuries of suicide in almost all cultures and civilisations, that this kind of avoidance does not work. Instead, avoidance, stigma and taboo increase the isolation and despair of people with thoughts of suicide and make suicide more likely.

When people are feeling the pain and despair of suicidal thoughts, and they believe that there is no one they can talk to about their feelings, they are at greater risk of acting on those thoughts.

People who are willing to talk about suicide in a direct, serious and open manner are rare, but they fulfil an important role. They make it possible for others to discuss suicide with them, and they make it clear by their attitude and willingness to talk that they are also willing to listen.

Suicide is a Serious Community Health Problem

The majority of people are not aware how common suicide is and how big a problem it is in the community. Making the mistake of believing that suicide is rare can lead us to assume that most of us do not need to do anything about it. Once we realise how common suicide is, it becomes clear that suicide prevention is everyone's business.

Other people
watch what we do

If they hear us talking about suicide in an open way, they may be more likely to come to us for help when they need it.

The Wider Impact of Suicide

Most people will be affected by suicide in some way during their lives.

Each year, death by suicide represents only a small part of the whole picture. Many more people attempt suicide than die by suicide. Research studies around the world estimate that for every one suicide, there are many times more attempted suicides that do not end in death. Research also shows that between 5% and 7% of people think about killing themselves each year. This amounts to over 250,000 people in Scotland each year with thoughts of suicide.[19]

Deaths by suicide, attempted suicide, and thoughts of suicide do not only affect the person themselves but also others around them. In some cases, the numbers of other people affected are relatively few. In other cases, for example the suicide of a high- profile person, a suicide in a public place or a school, hospital, prison or workplace, many people may be affected.

Suicide prevention is everyone's business

- On average, every day more than two people complete suicide in Scotland. This is more peoplethan die in road accidents.

- Suicide is a leading cause of death for people under 35, but it is not confined to this age group.

- Scotland's suicide rate is higher than any other part of the UK.

The Scottish Government: Suicide Prevention Strategy 2013–2016

There was a 19% fall in suicide rates between 2000–2 and 2011–13. This was just short of the Choose Life – National Strategy and Action Plan to Prevent Suicide in Scotland 10-year target to reduce suicides by 20% by 2013.

The new strategy to reduce suicide focuses on five key themes of work in communities and in services with 11 commitments to continue the downward trend in suicides and contribute to the delivery of the National Outcome to enable people to live longer, healthier lives.

The key themes are: responding to people in distress; talking about suicide; improving the NHS response to suicide; developing the evidence base; supporting change and improvement

To find out more visit the Choose Life website at www.chooselife.net

Anyone Can Have Thoughts of Suicide

Although people with certain characteristics may be more likely to have thoughts of suicide, no one is perfectly safe. The potential for thoughts of suicide is part of being human. Almost anyone can have thoughts of suicide at some time. This potential for having thoughts of suicide cannot be prevented, but suicidal acts that result in injury, pain and death can be. Most people thinking about suicide are not sure that they want to injure themselves, and most people who have thoughts of suicide do not act on the thoughts. Most people want help to stay alive.

Suicide, Mental Health Problems and Substance Misuse

Research has shown that mental health problems and substance misuse can make a person more vulnerable to suicide. This means that we should be aware of the possibility of suicidal thoughts if we are trying to help or support a person who has a mental health or substance misuse problem. However, it is important to remember that the absence of mental health or substance misuse problems does not eliminate the possibility of suicide.

Suicide is a separate issue from mental health problems, and from drug and alcohol misuse – even though these problems may make a person particularly vulnerable.

Why Offer First Aid?

There is a big difference between the things that cause a person to think about suicide and the decision to act on those thoughts.

A number of things may cause a person to have thoughts of suicide, such as negative life events, circumstances and individual resources. Personal tragedies or setbacks, bereavement, financial or personal problems can all cause a person to have thoughts of suicide. Some people appear to be more prone to thinking about suicide than others, and more easily experience feelings of despair. All these things have an impact on whether a person considers suicide.

The presence or absence of first aid help is critical to whether or not a person acts on their thoughts of suicide. By being there for a person who is having those thoughts you can save their life.

Personal health warning

Sometimes people choose to complete suicide regardless of whether or not we have offered to help them find an alternative. If this happens it is very important that we do not blame ourselves. Remember that you have tried to help in the best way you knew at the time. You do not have the power to change another person's mind. Only the person themselves can change their mind, others can offer to support them when they are distressed or in pain. Your positive intervention can give them an opportunity to consider their options. Similarly it is possible that while you are undertaking this training you begin to think about a time in the past when someone was thinking of suicide or acted on suicidal thoughts, and you didn't apply the steps you are learning about in this course. This course should never make you feel bad about yourself or about things you have done or not done in the past. We are not responsible for things we do not know. The best way to approach the learning in the course is to think of it as a way of acting in the future if you come across someone who is experiencing thoughts of suicide.

First Aid for **Suicide**

Ask about suicide

Listen non-judgmentally

Give reassurance and information

Encourage the person to get appropriate help

Encourage self-help strategies

step 1

Ask about suicide

> 'If you are worried that someone is suicidal,
> ask them. It could save their life.'

(Choose Life – A National Strategy and Action Plan to Prevent Suicide in Scotland 2003–13.)

Suicide is a life and death issue, so it takes priority and we need to check whether or not it is an issue for the person concerned.

Some facts on asking about suicide:

- Asking about suicide is not dangerous. You will not put the idea into a person's head by asking the question.

- People who are having suicidal thoughts often do not want to distress others by telling them how they are feeling. By asking the question, you are giving the person permission and inviting them to talk to you.

- People who are having suicidal thoughts are relieved when someone asks the question in a way that does not sound shocked or frightened.

- Your willingness to listen without judgment may save that person's life.

Therefore:

- If you suspect that someone might be thinking about suicide, ask them directly, clearly and as soon as possible.

- Do not let anything distract you from asking.

Because of the stigma and taboo around suicide, a person may not be able to say (unless they are invited to) that they are having thoughts of suicide. The person may instead show signs of distress. We can take these as indicators or invitations to ask them about thoughts of suicide. By then asking about suicide we give the person permission to talk about suicide.

Indicators or invitations to ask about suicide include:

- **Feelings:** desperate, angry, sad, ashamed, worthless, lonely, disconnected, hopeless.

- **Situations:** relationship problems, work problems, school, college or university problems, trouble with the law, family problems, abuse, suicide experience, addictions, physical health problems, mental health problems.

- **Thoughts:** escape, no future, guilty, alone, damaged, helpless, preoccupied, talk of suicide or death, planning for suicide.

- **Behaviours:** crying, emotional outbursts, alcohol or drug misuse, recklessness, fighting, law breaking, withdrawal, dropping out, prior suicidal behaviour, putting affairs in order, recent suicide attempt.

- **Physical changes**: lack of interest or pleasure, lack of physical energy, disturbed sleep, loss of sexual interest, loss of appetite, increase in minor illnesses.

- **Appearing more cheerful after distress:** Sometimes a person appears more cheerful after they have made the decision to end their lives. This is because they are anticipating the end of pain and feel relieved that the decision is made. This indicator is easily missed by friends and family because they are relieved to see their loved one appearing more cheerful.

This is not an exhaustive list. Often a person who has been trained to be aware of suicide risk will respond to a gut feeling rather than specific signs that a person is considering suicide. It is okay to listen to your gut feelings and ask the question if you are in any doubt at all. The best way to tell the difference between a person thinking about suicide and a person not thinking about suicide is to ask.

Getting it wrong

Imagine that something has caused you to think that suicide might be involved and you have decided to respond to it. What if you are wrong and the person does not have thoughts of suicide?

- **Suppose you are wrong and the person is not considering suicide.** What might happen? If you are wrong about suicide you have given the person an opportunity to talk about what might be troubling them. You have also shown that you care enough to ask the question.

- **Suppose you are right and the person is considering suicide.** You have made it possible for the person to talk about how they feel and to enable them to get appropriate help.

Suicide is about life and death. The best way to find out if a person is at risk is to ask.

Asking about suicide is a way of showing that you are concerned about the person and willing to help.

Imagine the scene:

A young woman is standing on the pier beside the sea. She appears wistful and seems to be thinking very seriously about something. Her demeanour is sad and she is standing very still. The coast guard sees her standing there and is concerned for her safety, so he approaches her and asks gently and kindly if she is okay, and then asks if she is considering suicide.

The young woman is startled because she hadn't been thinking about killing herself, but she has been sad and withdrawn because her marriage is in trouble. She has chosen to think about her options while she looks at the sea because she enjoys being near water and finds it restful.

When the coast guard approaches her and asks directly about suicide, she experiences a good feeling that someone cares enough to approach her and ask if she is alright. She thanks him for being concerned enough to ask and goes on her way feeling better about herself.

Finding a way to ask about suicide

One way of asking about suicide is to describe the indicators or invitations you have noticed and ask directly if they are connected to suicide.

You might say:

> 'When someone is (name the thing you
> have observed) they are sometimes thinking about
> suicide. Are you thinking about suicide?'

For example, if you are concerned that a person has thoughts of suicide because you heard them say there is no point going on, noticed that they were withdrawing from family and friends, and sensed that they were feeling hopeless, you would say:

> 'When someone is saying there is no point going
> on, feeling hopeless and withdrawing from family and
> friends they are sometimes thinking about suicide.
> Are you thinking about suicide?'

In the SMHFA training course you will get the chance to practise finding ways of posing the question in words that are comfortable for you.

Remember you need to use **very clear language.** This is not the time to use euphemisms, but rather to ask the question directly and kindly. For instance, it is not helpful to ask a question like, 'You are not thinking of doing something silly are you?' This is not a direct question and could have several meanings. The person may not be sure that you are really asking about their thoughts of suicide so they may hesitate to answer directly.

If the person answers 'no' to your direct question about thoughts of suicide and you believe them, then you have made it clear that you are willing to hear about whatever it is that is troubling them. They may or may not choose to talk to you, but you have made yourself available.

If they answer 'no' and you don't believe them, you can stay with them and keep listening to them until it is appropriate to ask again, or until you come to the conclusion that they are not considering suicide. If the person tells you that they do not want to talk to you it is important to accept it and respect their feelings. By doing this graciously and without a fuss you have made it clear that they can risk talking to you at another time.

Once you have asked the question, you need to be prepared for the answer.

How are you going to feel and react if the person says 'yes'?

This is an important moment and one you need to think about in advance so that you can help the person effectively.

When the person you are offering to help answers 'yes' to your question they will probably have mixed feelings. They may feel relief that you have asked them about the awful pain they are feeling, but they may also feel anxious that you will think badly of them.

Make it clear that you accept them without judgment by offering to listen to them in an open and non-judgmental way. Try not to act shocked or to recoil in horror. Stay calm and wait for them to say more.

step 2

Listen non-judgmentally

'Almost all persons at risk have not fully decided that they want to die. Most have not even decided that they don't want to live. Instead, they want to talk to someone about not wanting to live.'

(Suicide Talk: An Exploration in Suicide Awareness. LivingWorks 2004.)

- Encourage the person at risk to talk to you by being a good listener.

- It is possible that they have not talked to anyone about suicide, although they may have tried many times.

- Their talking to you can be very helpful, all by itself.

- People with thoughts of suicide have not usually fully decided that they want to die. Instead they want to talk to someone about not wanting to live.

- People with thoughts of suicide can talk themselves out of acting on their thoughts of suicide if they have someone who will really listen.

Listening is much more difficult than most of us realise. Most of the time we engage in conversation, which is a mixture of talking and listening. We talk about our own issues or interests and we will often be waiting politely for the other person to finish so that we can say our piece.

Another thing we often do when in conversation with a friend or family member who is telling us about their problems is to try to solve their problems for them. We tend to offer ideas – 'have you tried this?' or 'why don't you …'.

When we listen to someone who is having thoughts of suicide, we need to put aside this natural desire to solve their problems and allow them to get their feelings out in the open. We should listen in a way that is entirely focused on the person we are attempting to help. Giving full attention to what they are feeling and going through can be invaluable.

In the Mental Health First Aid course we go into listening skills in more depth in a later section (see page 52), but the key things to remember here are:

When listening

- Do not try to solve the person's problems.

- Do not argue or use guilt to try to get them to change their mind about suicide.

- Focus on the person and if unwanted feelings such as frustration or anger come into your mind, tell yourself that you will deal with them later, once you are out of the immediate situation.

- Try not to judge the person. You cannot fully know how bad they have been feeling and if the person senses your judgment or criticism they are likely to close up.

- Remember that by listening you are really helping.

Keep the person safe

When a person is having thoughts of suicide the single most important thing you can do is to keep that person safe until help arrives.

- Now is the time to do something that keeps the person at risk safe.

- Do not promise secrecy. You can promise discretion, sensitivity and a commitment to involve the person in decision making where possible, but not secrecy.

- Remove the means that might be used to complete a suicidal act.

- Get help from someone with suicide intervention skills by phoning a helpline such as Breathing Space, Samaritans or ChildLine, or contact local services such as ambulance, GP or mental health services.

If you believe the person you are helping is at risk of suicide, do not leave them alone. If possible take them to someone or ask someone else to bring help.

Keep yourself safe

You must always keep yourself safe. Never put yourself in danger – get or call for help instead.

step 3

Give reassurance and information

Tell the person that you will stay with them. This comforts and reassures the person.

Once the person has had a chance to talk to you about how they are feeling, you can reassure them that thoughts of suicide are common, but that most people who have thoughts of suicide recover and feel better relatively quickly. Explain that this is why you will stay with them and keep them safe until help arrives.

step 4

Encourage the person to get professional help

Once the immediate crisis is over, the person can get help for whatever the situation is that has caused the suicidal feelings to occur. You can tell the person this if they begin to ask what they are going to do about the problem or situation that has brought on the feelings.

step 5

Encourage self-help strategies

When a person is having thoughts of suicide, you can help by encouraging them to turn to someone they can trust to support them. Encourage the person to think of a person they can call on for help and support.

Alcohol will usually make thoughts of suicide worse and will cause the person's mood to be lower. If they are drinking, encourage them to stop and offer coffee, fruit juice or water and fresh air to help them sober up.

Self-care

Helping a person who is having thoughts of suicide can be rewarding and you can feel good about helping, but remember to take care of yourself too. After we have helped someone we can often feel stressed or distressed.

Looking after yourself is just as important as looking after others. There are many good stress-relieving techniques. Here are just a few:

- Talk to a friend
- Go for a brisk walk or take other exercise
- Breathing exercises, yoga or Tai Chi
- Listen to relaxing music
- Visualise a favourite place and imagine yourself there.

Learning More

The Suicide section in the SMHFA course is a brief introduction. If you would like to be more comfortable, confident and competent when helping a person with thoughts of suicide, you could attend safeTALK or ASIST.

safeTALK (Suicide Alertness for Everyone)

safeTALK was developed by LivingWorks Education. As more people are trained to be suicide alert, increasing numbers of people with thoughts of suicide are connected to the intervention help they need. In only a few hours, participants learn how to provide practical help to people with thoughts of suicide. Participants leave more willing, ready and able to perform an important role. By attending safeTALK you will:

- Understand that suicide is often missed, dismissed and avoided
- Examine the misleading ideas that stop us reaching out to help people with thoughts of suicide
- Learn and practice the TALK steps to notice when someone is at risk of suicide: ask directly about suicide, listen to what the person needs to say and link the person with an appropriate intervention service or source of help, e.g. someone trained in ASIST or with similar skills.

ASIST (Applied Suicide Intervention Skills Training)

ASIST is a LivingWorks Education programme that provides participants with the practical training to be more willing, ready and able to intervene in order to prevent the immediate risk of suicide.

Participants often include:

- People concerned about family or friends
- Helpers and advisers
- Emergency service workers
- Counsellors, teachers and ministers
- Mental health practitioners
- Workers in health, social care, welfare or justice
- Community volunteers.

The course is delivered over two consecutive days in a workshop format. It prepares caregivers to:

- Recognise the invitations for help
- Reach out and offer support
- Review the risk of suicide
- Apply a suicide intervention model
- Link people with community resources.

Evaluation has shown that the workshop increases participant's knowledge and confidence to respond to a person at risk of suicide. Intervention skills are retained over time, and are put to use to prevent the immediate risk of suicide.

For further information about safeTALK and ASIST and details of how to access these programmes, please visit the Choose Life website www.chooselife.net

Organisations

Breathing Space
www.breathingspace.scot
Tel: 0800 83 85 87

A confidential helpline for people to call when they are feeling down or distressed.

ChildLine
www.childline.org.uk
Tel: 0800 1111

Helpline for young people to discuss any problems or concerns.

Samaritans
www.samaritans.org
Tel: 116 123
Email: jo@samaritans.org

Talk things over in confidence with an experienced listener, or send an email.

In an emergency, do not hesitate to dial 999

Listening skills

AIMS of this **section**

- To learn and practice listening skills

- To understand that mental health first aid involves listening without discrimination.

How to Listen

To listen non-judgmentally is one of the five basic steps in SMHFA. It is a term that you will find used throughout this manual.

The course cannot train you to be a counsellor or a therapist, but you can develop some basic listening skills that will be useful in many situations.

Are You Really Listening?

Most of the time, we do not really listen to what others are saying. This is not because we are being rude or uncaring. Usually when we are in conversation with someone else, we find ourselves going off on other trains of thought because something that has been said has reminded us of other things. Other times we are thinking about our reply and only giving the speaker part of our attention.

When we are listening to the other person, part of our mind is thinking about our own reactions to what they are saying. This is a normal response, and in everyday situations, it usually works well.

In a situation where a person is distressed or having a mental health crisis, it is very important to pay more attention and put non-judgmental listening skills into practice.

Non-judgmental **listening** involves:

- Listening actively by doing all that you can to make sure you understand what the person is saying to you
- Resisting the urge to fix the person's problems by offering advice
- Putting aside your own feelings and attitudes temporarily, so that you can listen without judging the person
- Accepting the person exactly as they are
- Making no moral judgment about their situation
- Feeling and expressing genuine concern for the person.

Being an Effective Listener

While you are paying attention to the feelings of the other person, it is important to be aware of your own feelings and thoughts. Attending to a person who may be distressed may bring up a number of responses, such as fear, irritation, sadness, or a sense of being overwhelmed. These are normal responses to a difficult situation. However, it is important that the listener continues to be open to listening respectfully, and attempts to avoid reacting to what is being shared.

That means focusing on the distressed person, and understanding how it feels to be in their place.

This may be difficult, depending on the relationship between the listener and the distressed person. Sometimes it is especially difficult if the person is a close friend or relative. If you feel that your relationship is preventing you from being an effective listener, it may be best to get the help of someone else who is not so close to the person. However, in a crisis you may not have this option.

Remember that during a crisis, you are offering the distressed person a place of safety based on respect, acceptance and understanding – and you may be saving their life.

After the conversation, you may feel unsettled, shocked, confused, or angry. You may wish to share this with someone, to acknowledge your own experience. In doing so, you should maintain the person's privacy by withholding their name or any details that could identify them. This is not the same as accessing appropriate assistance for the person if they need it (e.g. if they are suicidal) when you will need to reveal their identity.

Always remember that you are human, and that feeling a mixture of emotions is a normal human response.

Overcoming Communication Difficulties

Communicating with people from different cultures
Any successful communication recognises the uniqueness of every culture, every relationship and every individual – including you.

Some forms of verbal and non-verbal communication are appropriate and others are not appropriate. For instance, some individuals may regard prolonged eye contact as rude. We all have different ways of communicating our fears and needs when we become unwell. Invite the person to tell you about their life experiences, values and belief systems. Also, ask them how they feel about asking for care and support.

Establish what is realistic for the individual, as well as what is culturally acceptable. Some cultures encourage the use of silence, whereas in others it others creates embarrassment or awkwardness. In some Islamic cultures, silence may indicate concern for privacy. In the French, Spanish and Soviet cultures, the presence of silence is a sign of agreement.

Working with an interpreter or a bilingual worker
When an individual does not speak English at all, has limited English, or chooses to communicate their distress in their mother tongue, the best solution is to use a professional interpreter. The choice to use a trained interpreter or a family member must be made by the individual who is experiencing problems. Being able to do so will help the individual to feel that he or she is in control of the situation.

Language holds and creates the individual's reality, experience, culture and world view. A good interpreter will concentrate on accurately conveying equivalent meaning as well as reporting the direct answers to your questions and other responses offered. You should also be aware that that the interpreter may bring his or her own bias to the situation.[20]

Working with a British Sign Language Interpreter for the deaf

There are very few services available for deaf people with mental health problems, although recently some deaf workers have been trained in SMHFA.

If no deaf mental health first-aider is available, you may need to use an interpreter. In this case, you should take care to always face the deaf person when speaking and respond as though it is the deaf person speaking to you when the interpreter speaks. Remember that the interpreter is being the deaf person's voice. Maintain good eye contact and show your feelings through your facial expressions. Deaf people do much of their communication through body language and facial expression, and are therefore skilled at reading feelings.

If no interpreter is available, you can still offer support and concern by showing your willingness to communicate. Deaf people can often lip read and can vocalise using English. Be patient and try hard to understand. Show your concern as you would with anyone in distress and ask the person who you can call for help.

Verbal skills

The skills you should use to show you are listening to the person are simple.

- Listen without interrupting.
- Pay attention.
- Ask appropriate questions to make sure that you are both clear on what is being said.
- Listen to the words and the tone of voice and look at the body language – all will give you clues as to how the person is feeling.
- Check your understanding of what is being said by saying something like 'It sounds like you are saying (or feeling)... have I understood that right?'

- Summarise facts and feelings. Minimal prompts such as, 'Mmm', 'Ah' or 'I see,' may be all that is necessary to keep the conversation going.

It is okay to have long pauses in the conversation. The person may simply be thinking or lost for words. If you say something to fill what you see as an embarrassing silence, you may break the train of thought or the rapport between you.

Sitting quietly, but attentively, through a period of silence will demonstrate that you value being with the other person. This is more effective than anything you may say will demonstrate.

Important note: If you need to use a pen and paper to ask the person who they would like you to call for help or support, use very simple English. British Sign Language is a different language to English – a person who was born deaf may not have English as their first language.

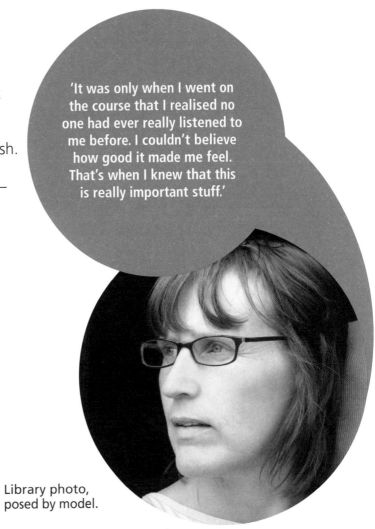

'It was only when I went on the course that I realised no one had ever really listened to me before. I couldn't believe how good it made me feel. That's when I knew that this is really important stuff.'

Library photo, posed by model.

Non-verbal skills (body language)

Make use of non-verbal communication skills:

- Be attentive
- Keep eye contact comfortable – do not stare or avoid eye contact
- Keep an open body position – try not to cross your arms across your body
- Sit down, even when the other person is standing – it will make you seem less threatening
- Try not to sit directly opposite, facing the other person – this may seem as though you are invading their space.

Self-harm

AIMS

of this section

- To understand self-harm

- To understand the differences and connections between self-harm and suicide

- To understand the risk factors for self-harm

- To be able to apply ALGEE when a person is self-harming

- To be aware of self-help strategies for self-harm.

Self-harm

Who me?

You smoke each day
Puff your life away
You clearly know it'll kill you

You drink with the moon
Drown your liver and soon
There's a chance it just may kill you

You drive too fast
And what if you crash?
You know it just might kill you

You smoke your dope
Take drugs, others hope
This time that they won't kill you

You over-eat
Can't see your feet
One day it'll certainly kill you

You look down on me
And all you can see
Are my cuts and scratches and scars

What you don't realise
Through those blinkered eyes
That mine are just skin deep

I'm living my life
While you're taking your life
Now tell me, who's the self-harmer?

Davina Smith
(with kind permission)

'I hope that one day people will understand that my self-harm is not about suicide and not wanting life. I self-harm because I want to be alive and sometimes hurting myself is the only thing that helps me hold on and stay in the world.' [21]

Library photo, posed by model.

Self-harm is not an illness. It is a behaviour that is used to either express or relieve feelings of distress. It is often not so much about inflicting pain on oneself as stopping emotional pain.

A common misunderstanding about self-harm is that it is a failed suicide attempt. In fact, most people who self-harm do so to cope with difficulties in their lives – rather than as a way to end their lives.

Self-harming behaviour can range from minor to serious injury. Many people who self-harm speak of a sense of control that the behaviour gives them. Some explain that physical pain is easier to deal with than emotional pain. Inflicting physical pain on oneself can mask the awareness of emotional pain for a short time. For some, self-harm is the only survival strategy they know, and therefore it is not helpful to try to get the person to stop the behaviour, without offering help to find new and less risky ways of coping.

Although the majority of people who self-harm have a strong desire to stay alive, some will be feeling suicidal. It is not that self-harm behaviour is of itself connected to the suicidal feelings, but rather that anyone who is experiencing mental pain or distress is at higher risk of suicidal thoughts or action.

This means that a mental health first-aider must keep both these facts in their minds when helping a person who self-harms.

- The person may be using self-harm as a way of coping.
- The person may be so distressed that they are at risk of suicide.

Any person who is experiencing mental distress or pain is at increased risk of suicide

This is similar to any other helping situation a mental health first-aider is involved in.

UK facts and figures
on self-harm [22]

- One in ten people aged 15 and 16 in the UK has self-harmed at some point in their life.

- Rates of self-harm in the UK are among the highest in Europe at 400 per 100,000 per year.

- Self-injury is uncommon in children under eleven, although there is evidence of children as young as five trying to harm themselves.

- Self-harm is three times more common among girls and young women than among boys and young men.

- It is possible that more men and boys self-harm than figures suggest.

- Of people who go to hospital because of self-harm, 15% will come back again for the same reason within a year.

Who is likely to self-harm?

- Negative childhood experiences may make a person more prone to self-harm. This might include bullying in school, bereavement or sexual abuse.

- Young South Asian women tend to self-harm more than other young women. This may be due to living in a racist society, as well as managing a dual identity of being both Asian and British.[23]

- Lesbian, gay and bisexual people are more likely to self-harm, because of the way society treats difference and because, even when one is aware of one's sexuality, it is difficult not to believe the negative ideas that surround you. This is called 'internalised homophobia' and it causes people to reject a part of themselves.[24]

- People who have had disadvantaged or deprived backgrounds are more likely to self-harm. It is vital not to overlook the fact that this also includes emotional deprivation, and may therefore be experienced in all income groups.

Some psychiatrists believe that self-harm is mainly used as a survival strategy – as a way to express unspoken emotions and to keep suicide impulses at bay. Some of the ways people might harm themselves include cutting or scratching the skin (particularly the arms), burning themselves, biting or punching themselves or hitting their body against something. Some people may swallow or insert objects into themselves; others may pull out their hair and eyelashes.

Self-harm is often done in secret and treatment of injuries is managed at home. This means that the reported figures do not represent the whole story.

Eating Disorders

Eating disorders are unlike other forms of self-harm because the impact of the behaviour is not instant. Very serious weight loss or weight gain, and other physical problems associated with eating disorders do not appear immediately and may not cause intense physical pain to the person.

Eating disorders can lead to death through starvation or poor nutrition. Some people with eating disorders also self-harm in the ways described above and need treatment for both problems.

People who starve themselves (anorexia) sometimes describe a feeling of control over the basic drive to eat. Others, particularly those who binge eat and vomit (bulimia), get comfort from overeating, and then vomit so that the large amount of food they have eaten does not cause them to gain weight.

Eating disorders are complex and require specialist care. There is a serious risk of sudden death through damage to major organs, or from a lack of essential vitamins and minerals.

Those trained in Mental Health First Aid should emphasise the need for specialist professional care for eating disorders and encourage the person to get the help they need. Listening without judgment will help gain the person's trust before suggesting the need for further help.

Reasons for self-harm

Most people who self-harm have had painful or traumatic experiences in their lives and have discovered self-harm as a way of coping with their distress. It is often associated with feelings of low self-esteem, guilt or self-blame.

If a person is unconsciously blaming themselves for an event in their lives, it is easier to understand why they might begin to hurt themselves. The initial pain gives them a feeling of control and relieves the feeling of being overwhelmed by painful or intense emotions. Sometimes, it also takes away feelings of emptiness or hopelessness.

Sudden intense pain can release endorphins, which are the body's natural pain reliever. This release of endorphins gives some people a feeling of temporary wellbeing. Some people report that self-harm helps them recover from feelings of dissociation or depersonalisation. In other words, when a person feels disconnected from what is going on around them, or feels that they are not really in the moment but looking on from a distance, they can feel more real or alive by inflicting pain on themselves.

Some can gain comfort from the self-care needed to manage their own physical wounds. This might indicate that the person has not learned to self-soothe in childhood, or has not been sufficiently comforted or cared for.

Self-harm is part of a recurring cycle of responses to 'triggers' in someone's life. These may include feeling inadequate, being rejected by someone important to them, or being blamed for something over which they have no control.

The majority of people find self-harm difficult to understand, yet for others it offers relief or comfort when they are very distressed. The mental health first-aider needs to put aside feelings of fear or horror if they are to offer help and comfort to a person who is self-harming.

Specific reasons vary from person to person

People may self-harm because they:

- Need a way to express their distress
- Need a respite from strong emotions like anger
- Need relief from tension and distress
- Feel it lets them escape from certain situations in their lives
- Need to relieve feelings of numbness
- Need attention
- Are under strain from peer pressure
- Are influenced by the example of role models.

The Attention Seeking Question

Many people lack empathy or patience with people who self-harm because they believe it to be attention-seeking behaviour.

'Attention seeking' is a term used in British culture to dismiss other people's behaviour as inappropriate or childish. Most of us have negative ideas about attention seeking, and we would feel insulted or hurt if someone accused us of behaving in such a way.

Perhaps it is time to unpack the whole idea.

Human beings need attention. Babies who do not receive enough physical and emotional attention become very unwell. Children need attention in order to flourish and face the world with confidence and a good sense of self. Young people need attention in order to negotiate the difficult shift from childhood to adulthood and as they develop their own identity. Adults need attention in order to maintain self-esteem, and to feel emotionally and mentally well.

If anyone is deprived of attention, it has a negative effect on their mental health.

We all need attention, and we seek what we need as part of our survival. What this means is that everyone seeks attention in some way. Attention-seeking behaviour is often both normal and appropriate.

Interestingly, people who self-harm often do so in secret and never tell anyone about it. In other words, they try very hard not to draw attention to their self-harming behaviour. This may be due to the realisation that others will judge them or it may be that they do not want to hurt or distress those closest to them. The secretive nature of most self-harm suggests that it is not usually attention-seeking behaviour. It is often used as a means of meeting some other urgent need on the part of the person who is self-harming.

Some people do self-harm as a means of drawing attention to their pain, and in this case they may do so because they have found that using words has not worked or is too difficult. When this is the case, the person is seeking the attention that they need as a human being, and it is important that someone responds with care and concern.

What is needed here is for someone to pay attention, and in doing so, the road to recovery for the person in distress might begin.

Recovery

Self-harming behaviour can be reduced with appropriate support. Hope for improvement and control in the lives of people who self-harm can be very important in reducing and eventually stopping the self-harm. Most people stop harming themselves when they are ready to do so, and by finding other ways of dealing with their feelings. It might take a long time, but people can and do recover.

First Aid for **Self-harm**

Ask about suicide
Listen non-judgmentally
Give reassurance and information
Encourage the person to get appropriate help
Encourage self-help strategies

step 1

Ask about suicide

People who self-harm need to be monitored closely. Self-harm is a serious problem that can cause disability and death. People who self-harm are at an increased risk of suicide. Even if the person does not intend to die, they can kill themselves by accident. About two percent of those who self-harm will kill themselves within one year.

A person who is self-harming may be so distressed that they are considering suicide. Fuller guidance is available in the Suicide section of the manual, see page 38.

step 2

Listen non-judgmentally

> 'My hope is that anyone experiencing thoughts of self-harm, or who goes into self-harm, has someone to talk to and does not feel isolated.' [21]

Self-harm can be hard for a person to talk about. They may be afraid of how others will react. It is best to respond calmly and to avoid anger or judgment so that the person remains willing to discuss their self-harming behaviour. The person should never be dismissed as manipulative or attention seeking.

The person who self-harms is genuinely distressed, and they are not managing to cope with this distress. They need to be listened to and supported without judgment.

Many people who self-harm have never had the chance to talk to another person without being asked to stop their self-harming behaviour. Some support agencies in the past have demanded that a person stops self-harming before they can be helped.

This is not helpful because self-harm is often the only coping mechanism the person has learned.

When listening to the person:
- Listen without asking 'why?'
- Listen without suggesting ways to fix the problem
- Listen without appearing shocked
- Listen with genuine concern for the person's feelings.

step 3

Give reassurance and information

Once you have listened without judgment and without problem solving, you can try to help the person to realise that there may be underlying problems that can be helped. These problems may be emotional, social, physical or mental. Asking for help may be the first step towards recovery.

Most people who self-harm do not seek any professional help. Encouraging them to talk to people they can trust, like a family member, a friend or teacher, a social worker, counsellor or doctor. Sometimes it is easier to talk to a stranger, perhaps someone from the organisations listed in Helpful Resources on page 68.

step 4

Encourage the person to get professional help

The sources of professional help rated most satisfactory by people who self-harm are GPs, psychiatrists, psychologists or counsellors. Many people who self-harm have an underlying mental health problem, and these professionals can look for any problems and treat them.

Treatment and help for mental health problems is possible and effective, so it is important to encourage the person who self-harms to ask for that help. This may be difficult because of embarrassment, shame or fear of ridicule.

If a person has minor wounds, these can be treated without medical help. However, if a person has overdosed or has injuries that are putting them at risk, it is important to call an ambulance or to take them to the emergency department of a hospital as soon as possible. In Accident and Emergency departments across Scotland there are increasing numbers of specialist self-harm nurses. This initiative will help people get the care they need.

People who self-harm may find it difficult to consistently attend appointments given to them for ongoing care. A mental health first-aider can make a big difference by encouraging the person to go to appointments or even consider going with them to support them.

step 5

Encourage self-help strategies

Meeting others with similar experiences of self-harm can be very helpful. Support groups can provide a valuable opportunity to talk about feelings without having to explain or justify. There are also many books and websites that may help, and a number of useful telephone helplines. Some chat rooms can be helpful, but others encourage self-harm. Make certain that any web address you offer to the person has been properly vetted. There is a list of appropriate sites at the end of this section.

Being creative can help express feelings in a non-verbal way. Other relaxing distractions might include listening to relaxing music or watching a non-violent DVD, doing housework or going shopping, exercising, walking, baking or cooking a meal. Relaxation techniques like yoga and meditation also help. Alcohol and drugs should be avoided since they can cause more impulsive actions and increase the risk of self-harming.

Organisations

Scottish Association for Mental Health (SAMH)
www.samh.org.uk
Tel: 0141 530 1000

Works to support people who experience mental health problems, homelessness, addictions and other forms of social exclusion.

Penumbra
www.penumbra.org.uk
Tel: 0131 475 2380

Works to provide a wide range of mental health support services for adults and young people.

Fife Early Response Self-harm Project
Tel: 01383 747788

Works to provide an early response support service to people over 18 who have been involved in a self-harming incident.

Scottish Recovery Network
www.scottishrecovery.net
Tel: 0141 240 7790
Email: info@scottishrecovery.net

Promotes and supports recovery from long-term mental health problems in Scotland.

Library and Knowledge Services
www.healthscotland.com/resources/library/index.aspx
Tel: 0141 414 2762
Email: nhs.healthscotland-knowledge@nhs.net

Knowledge Services is a national resource for anyone interested in improving population health and reducing health inequalities in Scotland.

Our services are aimed at helping you access high-quality, relevant evidence across a range of themes.

Eating Disorders Association
www.b-eat.co.uk
Tel: 0345 634 1414
Email: help@b-eat.co.uk

Information and help on all aspects of eating disorders, including anorexia nervosa, bulimia nervosa and binge-eating disorder.

Additional Websites

www.selfinjurysupport.org.uk
Works to support girls and women in emotional distress, and to develop services and raise awareness of self-harm and mental health issues.

www.selfharm.co.uk
Provides self-harm recovery, advice and support for young people.

www.mind.org.uk
Works to create a better life for everyone with experience of mental distress.

www.thecalmzone.net
Targeted at young men aged between 15-35, offering help, information and advice. Anyone, regardless of age, gender or geographic location can call the helpline.

www.sane.org.uk
Works to raise awareness and respect for people with mental illness and their families, and to secure better services.

www.samaritans.org

Confidential emotional support, 24 hours a day, for people who are experiencing feelings of distress or despair, including those which could lead to suicide.

www.breathingspace.scot

A confidential helpline service for any individual who is experiencing low mood or depression.

www.nshn.co.uk

The National Self-harm Network, providing a forum for survivors, professionals and family.

www.recoveryourlife.com

Online self-harm support community.

Additional Reading

Talking about self-harm.

Part of the 'Talking About' series of leaflets. www.healthscotland.com/documents/27.aspx
Edinburgh: NHS Health Scotland, 2015
ISBN 1-84485-302-1

Depression

AIMS

of this **section**

- To understand the term 'depression'

- To understand how having depression affects a person's life

- To gain knowledge about the impact of alcohol and drugs on depression

- To be able to apply ALGEE when helping a person who appears to be depressed

- To know where further help can be found.

What is Depression?

The word 'depression' is used in many different ways. Everyone can feel sad or blue when bad things happen. However, everyday blues or sadness is not depression. People may have a short-term depressed mood, but they can manage to cope and soon recover without treatment. The SMHFA course is concerned with major depression.

A major depression is one that lasts for at least two weeks, affects the person's behaviour, and also has physical, emotional and cognitive effects. It interferes with the ability to work and to have satisfying personal relationships.

Depression is a common but serious illness that affects around 7 in every 100 adults in Scotland in any year. A person can have just one, or several, episodes of depression throughout their life. Depression also occurs with other mental health problems and with physical illnesses such as coronary heart disease, stroke, diabetes and physical disabilities.

Although depression is considered an illness in some cultures, in others it is thought of differently. Some cultures view low mood as related to the person's spiritual life rather than mental health. Other cultures do not recognise the concept of depression at all.

Symptoms of Depression

A person who is clinically depressed will have at least two of the following symptoms for at least two weeks:

- An unusually sad mood that does not go away
- Loss of enjoyment and interest in activities that used to be enjoyable
- Lack of energy and tiredness.

People who are depressed can also have other symptoms, such as:

- Loss of confidence in themselves, or poor self-esteem
- Feeling guilty when they are not at fault
- Wishing they were dead
- Difficulty in concentrating or making decisions
- Moving more slowly or being agitated and unable to settle
- Having difficulty sleeping or sleeping too much
- Loss of interest in food, or eating too much – possibly resulting in weight loss or gain.

Not every person who is depressed has all these symptoms. People who are more severely depressed will have more symptoms than those who are mildly depressed. Here is a guide to severity of depression:

- Mild depression – four of the ten symptoms over the past two weeks
- Moderate depression – six of the ten symptoms over the past two weeks
- Severe depression – eight of the ten symptoms over the past two weeks.

Effects of Depression

Depression affects emotions, thinking, behaviour and physical wellbeing, and impacts individuals in different ways. Some examples are:

- **Effects on emotion**: sadness, anxiety, guilt, anger, mood swings, lack of emotional responsiveness, helplessness, hopelessness.

- **Effects on thinking**: frequent self-criticism, self-blame, worry, pessimism, impaired memory and concentration, difficulty making decisions, confusion, a tendency to believe others see them in negative light, thoughts of death and suicide.

- **Effects on behaviour**: crying spells, withdrawal from others, neglect of responsibilities, loss of interest in personal appearance, loss of motivation.

- **Physical effects**: chronic fatigue, lack of energy, sleeping too much or too little, overeating or loss of appetite, constipation, weight loss or gain, irregular menstrual cycle, loss of sexual desire, unexplained aches and pains.

- **Cultural issues**: people from different cultural backgrounds may express the signs and symptoms of depression through feelings of isolation, shame or guilt, or in physical terms.

Summary of a depressed person

A person who is depressed may:
- Look sad, depressed and anxious
- Be slow in moving and thinking
- Speak in a slow and monotonous way
- Look unkempt
- Be irritable and easily moved to tears.

In severe depression, the person often describes being emotionally blunted and 'beyond tears'. There may be a lack of attention to physical appearance and personal hygiene. While depressed people will often be slow in moving and thinking, they may also become agitated from time to time.

Attitudes and Thinking

Depressed people commonly have a negative view of themselves, the world and their future. Their thoughts often follow themes of hopelessness and helplessness. They may say things such as:

- 'I'm a failure'
- 'I have let everyone down'
- 'It's all my fault'
- 'Nothing good ever happens to me'
- 'I'm worthless'
- 'No one loves me'
- 'I am so alone'
- 'Life is not worth living'
- 'There is nothing good out there'
- 'Things will always be bad'

Bipolar disorder is a depressive illness in which the person experiences severe episodes of depression as well as episodes of mania. During these episodes of mania, the person is likely to experience symptoms of psychosis. Further details of bipolar disorder can be found in the Psychosis section of the manual, see page 108.

Risk factors for depression

Depression has no single cause and often involves different physical, psychological and social factors. People can become depressed when something very distressing has happened to them and they cannot do anything to control the situation.

Examples include:

- The break-up of a relationship or living in conflict
- Loss of a job and difficulty in finding a new one
- Having an accident which results in a long-term disability
- Being the victim of a crime
- Developing a long-term physical illness
- Caring full time for someone with a long-term disability
- Unresolved bereavement, particularly in childhood.

Depression can also result from:

- Some medical conditions, such as stroke, dementia, hypothyroidism, Cushing's disease, Addison's disease and Parkinson's disease
- Having a baby (10-15% of women develop depression shortly after childbirth)
- The side effects of certain medications or drugs
- The stress of having another mental illness such as schizophrenia or severe anxiety

Alcohol and Depression

It is widely recognised that alcohol makes mental health problems worse. Alcohol is a depressant drug. Depressant drugs interfere with and slow the operation of the central nervous system (other depressants include the drugs we call tranquillisers). Alcohol intensifies mood, so a depressed person is likely to feel worse under the influence of alcohol. Alcohol also disrupts sleep patterns and so can contribute to depression by increasing fatigue.

Some people use alcohol to get relief from their symptoms. In the short term, the physical effects of hangovers and the low mood states they bring make life harder to cope with. In the longer term, the negative effects of alcohol on physical health, finances and relationships place extra strain on the person. This makes recovery from depression even more difficult. If a person is having thoughts of suicide, they are more likely to act on their thoughts if they have been drinking.

Alcohol and Medication for Depression

Alcohol reacts badly with many psychiatric drugs, including some used to treat depression. It stops some anti-psychotic drugs, used to treat the mania of bipolar disorder, from working properly. This means that a person who drinks may need higher doses of these medications. Taking any medication at higher doses increases the risk of negative side effects.

- The stress of alcohol or drug dependency
- Premenstrual and menopausal changes in hormone levels
- Lack of exposure to sunlight in the winter months.

Some people will develop depression as a result of a distressing situation, whereas others in the same situation will not.

Those most prone to developing depression are: [25]

- Women
- People who have a history of depression in their family
- People who have had a difficult childhood (for example, physical abuse, neglect, overly strict, early bereavement)
- People who experience harassment, such as bullying, discrimination or oppression in the form of sexism or racism.

Alcohol can cause poisoning or extreme sleepiness in people taking different forms of antidepressants. Other drugs used to treat mental health problems may also react badly to alcohol. It is always important that people let their doctor know how much alcohol they drink so that they can be prescribed appropriate types and dosages of drugs.

Illegal or Recreational Drugs and Depression

People with drug and alcohol problems have higher rates of other mental health problems. As with alcohol, some people use illegal drugs to try to gain relief from their symptoms of depression. (See the Alcohol and Drug section on page 30 for further information on the debate on cannabis use and the development of mental ill health, including depression.)

For a depressed person, the use of ecstasy and other stimulants can seem like opening a window in a darkened room. However, the reverse is also true of the after-effects of using the drug. The 'low' or 'come-down' from ecstasy involves:

- Immediately afterwards, users may be unable to sleep properly

- For two to three days after using it, users report feeling very down or low.

'When I was depressed I was constantly worrying that I had said or done the wrong thing. I used to come home and worry about things that had happened. Then I would give myself a telling-off for being stupid! I didn't know it was depression. I just thought I had lost confidence and couldn't work out why.'

For these reasons, using ecstasy is not helpful to people with mood disorders. This may be particularly true for someone with bipolar disorder, in which recovery involves trying to smooth out the highs and lows in the swings from mania to depression.

Ecstasy usually comes in the form of a pill, and is often mixed with amphetamines and other illegal drugs. These have added dangers for people with mental health problems.

Some research has suggested that repeated or heavy use of ecstasy damages the brain's ability to respond to natural brain chemicals that lift mood. It may therefore contribute to the development of depression and other mood disorders. The long-term effects of using ecstasy are not fully understood.[26]

Library photo, posed by model.

First Aid for **Depression**

Ask about suicide

Listen non-judgmentally

Give reassurance and information

Encourage the person to get appropriate help

Encourage self-help strategies

step 1

Ask about suicide

The symptoms of depression can make a person feel so overwhelmed and helpless that the future appears hopeless. They may think suicide is the only solution. Depression is a major risk factor for suicide, although not everyone who attempts suicide is depressed. If you think someone may be having thoughts of suicide, work through the steps below.

- Engage the person in a serious conversation about how they are feeling. For example, you might ask if they are experiencing a crisis in their lives. Are they feeling hopeless or helpless? Have they withdrawn from their usual activities? Have they started risk-taking behaviour? Let them describe how they are feeling. Be aware of any cultural context that may have an impact on why the person is feeling this way now.

- Identify if the person is at risk. Ask them 'Are you having thoughts of suicide?' This type of questioning does not encourage people to pursue suicidal behaviour. Rather, it signals that you care, and that you realise they may be considering suicide. They will know that you are ready to talk with them about it. The opportunity to discuss the feelings and emotions surrounding thoughts of suicide is often a great relief to people.

- Find out about their available support structure. If a person feels totally alone and without any resources they are at greater risk of attempting suicide.

Ask them:

- 'Who do you feel most able to ask for help or support?'
- 'Is there anyone you would like me to call?'

All feelings of distress should be taken seriously.

If you believe the person you are helping is at risk of suicide do not leave them alone. Refer to the Suicide section on page 38.

step 2

Listen non-judgmentally

A person who is feeling depressed may benefit from being able to talk about how they feel, especially if the helper can listen without judging or offering advice. Always accept the person's feelings as real to them and do not try to argue or jolly them out of their low mood.

- Listen to the person without judging them as weak.
- Do not try to jolly them along with humour.
- Remember that these problems are not due to weakness or laziness. The person is unwell and is trying to cope.
- Do not be critical.
- Do not express frustration to the person for having such symptoms.
- Do not offer advice such as 'pull yourself together' or 'cheer up'.
- Avoid confrontation unless necessary to prevent harmful or dangerous acts.

Refer to the Listening Skills section on page 52.

step 3

Give reassurance and information

Help the person to feel hopeful and optimistic by telling them that:

- Depression is a common illness
- Depression is not a weakness or character defect
- Effective treatments are available for depression
- Your GP can help

- There are some things you can do in the short term to make yourself feel better
- Depression is not laziness – depression takes away energy and motivation
- Depression takes a while to develop and can take time to resolve, but it will get better faster with the right help.

step 4

Encourage the person to get professional help

Sometimes when people are depressed they feel anxious about asking for professional help. This may be because of a fear of getting a diagnosis of a mental health problem, concern about being admitted to hospital or a fear of the side effects of medication.

The majority of people who are diagnosed with a mental health problem are treated by their GP, and remain at home. Only a very small number of people who are very seriously ill are admitted to hospital for treatment.

When depression is severe it is not unusual for care to be provided by a team of professionals including GPs, psychiatrists, counsellors, psychologists, community psychiatric nurses (CPN) and members of voluntary sector organisations. Hospital chaplains may be involved in offering support to people of faith who are experiencing depression.

Getting Professional Help

GPs
Many people with depression will approach their GP for professional help in the first instance.

The GP will ask the person some questions, using a recognised tool designed to work out how severe the person's depression is. After this, she or he is likely to take a 'stepped-care approach' to treatment.

This method of treatment is taken from the National Institute for Clinical Excellence (NICE), 2011 guidelines. This involves clinically-proven, best-practice pathways to care through a series of steps that recognise patient choice and preference.

These steps involve:

- 'Watchful waiting' – which means asking the person to come regularly to discuss how they are feeling. The reason for taking this initial approach is that some people who experience a bout of depression recover naturally in a few weeks

- The use of guided self-help and other brief therapies. This can be used at the same time as watchful waiting, and might include using self-help books or prescribed exercise

- If the first two treatments are not helping, the person will be offered psychological therapies and/or medication

- Finally, the person may be offered treatment by a psychiatrist if the earlier treatments were not successful.[25]

The benefit of the stepped-care approach is that the depressed person can be offered a range of different treatments. They also have more say in their own treatment, and therefore have a better chance of recovery.

GPs can make a quicker diagnosis if the person tells them directly that they believe that they are depressed. Some GPs are more comfortable dealing with depression than others. However, a GP should take the time to listen to the person and take account of the person's treatment preferences. If a person is not happy with a particular GP, they should not hesitate to seek help from a different GP where one is available.

Community Psychiatric Nurses

The Community Psychiatric Nurse (CPN) is part of the local community mental health team, and is trained to support and care for people with a diagnosis of a mental illness in their own home or at a local clinic. CPNs are experienced psychiatric nurses and may be trained in cognitive behaviour therapy (CBT) or other forms of therapy. The CPN will advise on medication and on finding ways to manage symptoms.

Counsellors and Clinical Psychologists

Counsellors and clinical psychologists specialise in the psychological treatment of mental health problems. They are not medically qualified and so they cannot prescribe antidepressants or other drugs. Counsellors and psychologists vary a lot in their level of training and in their experience of helping people with depression.

A counsellor or clinical psychologist can help by providing:

- Opportunities to talk about problems
- Opportunities to be listened to in an emotionally supportive and non-judgmental way
- Specific methods for overcoming depression and preventing its recurrence.

A good counsellor or clinical psychologist will use methods to promote coping, such as CBT or interpersonal psychotherapy. Many qualified counsellors will be registered with organisations such as Counselling and Psychotherapy in Scotland (COSCA) or the British Association for Counselling and Psychotherapy (BACP).

Cognitive behaviour therapy (CBT) is based on the idea that how we think affects the way we feel. When people get depressed they think negatively about most things. There may be thoughts of how hopeless their situation is and how helpless they feel. They can have a negative view of themselves, the world and their future. Cognitive behaviour therapy helps people to recognise such unhelpful thoughts and change them to more realistic ones. Access to CBT is improving as more health workers are being trained in its use.

Interpersonal psychotherapy is a short-term therapy that focuses on the relationships in a person's life and the way these relationships affect the person's wellbeing. It may focus on the way the person relates to others or it may help the person work through relationship problems either from the past or in the present.

Psychodynamic psychotherapy helps the person understand some of the unconscious or hidden processes that are causing problems in the present. These may be based on early childhood experiences or issues to do with parents, some of which may have been forgotten. The therapist may also analyse the way in which the client relates to them, thereby helping the person recognise old patterns of behaviour of which they are not aware.

If a person wants help from a counsellor or clinical psychologist, they can either contact one directly (counsellors and clinical psychologists are listed in the telephone directory) or get a recommendation from a GP. Several organisations have nationwide lists of therapists. See 'Finding a Therapist' in the Helpful Resources on page 86.

Psychiatrists

Psychiatrists are medical specialists who treat mental health problems. They are experts on medication. They can prescribe drugs, and help people who are having side effects from their medication or negative interactions with other medications. Psychiatrists can also be helpful to people who have depression combined with other medical problems. Psychiatrists can only be seen by referral from a GP. The GP might refer a patient to a psychiatrist if he or she is very ill or not getting better.

Only in the most severe cases of depression, or where there is a danger a person might cause harm to themselves or others, is a depressed person admitted to hospital. Most people with depression are treated successfully in the community.

The Voluntary Sector

The voluntary sector is an integral part of mental health care in the community. Voluntary sector organisations provide a range of services including:

- Help with daily living
- Befriending or visiting services
- Advice and information
- Help with mobility and transport
- Counselling or other therapies
- Self-help and support groups
- Supported employment.

Voluntary sector organisations may already be involved in supporting the person, regardless of their mental health status. The services offered differ from area to area. To find out what is available, consult your local volunteer centre or look in the Yellow Pages under 'voluntary organisations'.

Telephone Helplines

Opportunities to talk are always available over the telephone. Some organisations also offer email helplines. See 'National Telephone Support' in the Helpful Resources listings on page 86.

Encourage self-help strategies

A number of self-help techniques are very effective. As well as having proven benefits, self-help strategies help people to feel that they are regaining control of their lives and doing something positive for themselves. Depression support groups can be a useful source of mutual support and information. Contact details for organisations with directories of local self-help groups are listed under Helpful Resources overleaf.

Family and friends are a very important source of support for a person who is depressed. People who feel supported by those around them recover faster. Family and friends can help by:

- Listening to the person with depression without judging or being critical

- Encouraging the person to get appropriate professional help

- Checking if the person is feeling suicidal and, if so, taking immediate action

- Providing the same support as for a physically ill person (e.g. sending get well cards or flowers, telephoning or visiting, helping out when the person cannot manage).

St. John's Wort: This is a naturally occurring herbal remedy that has been found to help mild depression. Before taking St John's Wort, you should ask your pharmacist or doctor for advice as it can interact with other drugs, including the contraceptive pill and other antidepressants.[27, 28]

Exercise: Exercise has great benefits for depression and anxiety. The release of 'feel good' brain chemicals lift low mood, and help the person sleep well. Improved physical fitness also positively affects mental wellbeing.[29]

Light therapy: People who experience low mood in winter can be helped by the proper use of light therapy. Lamps that provide the same kind of light as sunshine raise mood and aid better sleep.[30]

Social interventions: There is a good deal of evidence to suggest that social capital both protects against ill health and helps people recover from it. Social capital is the extent to which a person is involved in social relationships and feels a sense of belonging and identity in the local community.[31]

Acupuncture,[32] massage therapy,[33] relaxation therapy,[34] and yoga breathing exercises[35] are all effective treatments to aid low mood.

Cognitive behaviour therapy (CBT): [36] Has been found to be very effective for depression in some people. People who are feeling depressed tend to view situations in a negative way and make negative assumptions. For instance, a person who is depressed may feel that no one likes them based on an offhand conversation with a friend, colleague or family member. Although these are described as feelings, they are actually based on thoughts, e.g. 'I think he doesn't like me anymore' or 'He wasn't paying attention to what I was saying so I think he doesn't like me anymore'. These thoughts come from the way the conversation or situation has been interpreted. Once the thoughts take hold, the person begins to feel depressed or upset.

CBT can help a person learn new ways of interpreting situations and ways of stopping the negative thoughts from taking hold. This then relieves feelings of depression.

Reading self-help books based on CBT and working through CBT exercises online are both very effective ways of using CBT without the need for a professional therapist. CBT is one way in which a GP can offer early treatment to a person with depression.

Living Life to the Full is a Scottish web-based CBT treatment site that is free to use. Visit **www.livinglifetothefull.com**

Other effective forms of psychotherapy are described on page 81.

Medical treatments for depression: There are a number of different antidepressants that may be used for moderate to severe depression, often alongside other treatments such as CBT and exercise. There is some evidence to suggest that antidepressants may be unhelpful in young people and will only be offered to under 18s in more severe cases and alongside other treatments such as CBT.[37]

Organisations

Action on Depression
www.actionondepression.org

Provides information and support to people with depression and their carers, and also lists details of local self-help groups.

Bipolar Scotland
www.bipolarscotland.org.uk
Tel: 0141 560 2050

Works to provide information, support and advice for people affected by bipolar disorder and their carers.

Scottish Recovery Network
www.scottishrecovery.net
Tel: 0141 240 7790
Email: info@scottishrecovery.net

Promotes and supports recovery from long-term mental health problems in Scotland.

Scottish Association for Mental Health (SAMH)
www.samh.org.uk
Tel: 0141 530 1000

Works to support people who experience mental health problems, homelessness, addictions and other forms of social exclusion.

MIND
www.mind.org.uk

Works to create a better life for everyone with experience of mental distress. Depression and manic depression fact sheets can be downloaded from the website.

DIPEx
www.healthtalk.org

Watch, listen and read interviews with people who have personal experience of depression, and find reliable information on treatment and where to find support.

ASIST (Applied Suicide Intervention Skills Training)
www.chooselife.net

A two-day training course that teaches people how to intervene when someone is suicidal. The courses are organised by the Choose Life programme. See the Learning More resources in the Suicide section, on page 50.

MoodJuice
www.moodjuice.scot.nhs.uk

Provides self-help resources, information, and advice to those experiencing troublesome thoughts, feelings and actions. Also for carers and professionals.

Doing Well
www.doingwell.org.uk

A website that gives users the opportunity to measure their own level of depression and to find out what help is available.

First aid
www.firstaid.org.uk

Provides information on general first aid training courses – including how to provide first aid when someone is unconscious.

Living Life to the Full
www.llttf.com

A Scottish interactive site for depression and anxiety, where users can access cognitive behaviour therapy (CBT) treatments online.

Mood Gym
www.moodgym.anu.edu.au

An interactive site that teaches people to use ways of thinking that will help to prevent depression, based on cognitive behaviour therapy (CBT).

The South Glasgow Wellbeing Services

http://wellbeing-glasgow.org.uk

Provides a range of self-help information and materials, based on cognitive behaviour therapy (CBT).

National Telephone Support

Breathing Space

www.breathingspace.scot
Tel: 0800 83 85 87

A confidential helpline for people to call when they are feeling down or distressed.

Samaritans

www.samaritans.org
Tel: 116 123
Email: jo@samaritans.org

Talk things over in confidence with an experienced listener, or send an email.

Finding a Therapist

Counsellors and psychotherapists are listed in the Yellow Pages. The following organisations also have national lists of therapists:

The British Psychological Society

www.bps.org.uk
Tel: 0116 254 9568

British Association for Behavioural and Cognitive Therapists

www.babcp.com
Tel: 0161 705 4304

COSCA – Counselling and Psychotherapy in Scotland

www.cosca.org.uk
Tel: 0178 647 5140

British Association for Counselling and Psychotherapy

www.bacp.co.uk
Tel: 0145 588 3300

Self-help Groups

For listings of local self-help groups for depression, see the Depression Alliance, and for bipolar disorder (manic depression), see the Bipolar Fellowship Scotland (above).

Self-help Books

Tanner, S. and Ball, J. (1991). *Beating the Blues.* **Southwood Press: Sydney.**

A very readable step-by-step programme using cognitive behaviour therapy (CBT).

Williams, C. (2004). *Overcoming Depression: A Five Areas Approach.* **Arnold: London.**

A self-help manual based on cognitive behaviour therapy (CBT).

Copeland, M.E. and McKay, M. (2002). *The Depression Workbook: A Guide for Living with Depression and Manic Depression.* **New Harbinger Publications: Oakland, CA.**

Based on extensive research, this book contains interactive exercises that provide guidance on essential coping skills, to help readers make real changes in their lives.

Additional Reading

Talking about Depression.

Part of the 'Talking About' series of leaflets. www.healthscotland.com/documents/1017.aspx
Edinburgh: NHS Health Scotland, 2015
ISBN 978-1-84485-346-5

Johnstone, N. (2003). *A Head Full of Blue.* **Bloomsbury: London.**

A personal account of the effects of suffering from depression, anxiety disorder and alcoholism.

Matthew, J. (2007). *I Had a Black Dog*. Constable: London

There are many different breeds of black dog affecting millions of people from all walks of life. The black dog is an equal opportunity mongrel.

Other Information

NICE (National Institute for Clinical Excellence in the NHS in England and Wales)
www.nice.org.uk

Anxiety

AIMS

of this **section**

- To understand the nature of anxiety
- To know the difference between anxiety and an anxiety disorder
- To understand the various types of anxiety disorders
- To be able to apply ALGEE when a person is experiencing anxiety
- To know some immediate self-help strategies for anxiety.

Anxiety

Anxiety is a normal reaction that is necessary to keep us safe. Feelings of anxiety prevent us from taking risks and from acting on impulse. Anxiety becomes a problem when it interferes with a person's ability to work, have relationships or socialise with others.

Feeling anxious is unpleasant for a reason. It causes us to take notice of our feelings and therefore avoid dangerous situations. Feelings of anxiety are related to a very basic mechanism that is sometimes called the 'fight or flight response'. The fight or flight response has been part of the physical and psychological makeup of humans and animals throughout history.

Fight or Flight

Imagine yourself stepping out into a busy street only to see a huge lorry approaching you at speed. What do you do? You leap back onto the pavement with a speed and agility you would find impossible to match elsewhere. Your body has shifted up a gear and provided you with the energy it needs to save itself. Once you are safely on the pavement and the lorry has rushed by, you will probably feel breathless, shaky, frightened, tearful, sweaty, in need of the toilet, dry mouthed, pale faced and you may even feel sick.

The reason you feel all these physical sensations is that your brain has triggered a series of physical responses. Blood has changed course from the surface of your skin to the large muscles in your arms and legs to supply extra oxygen. Your heart is pumping much faster to get the blood to those muscles as quickly as possible, therefore making you pale and breathless. Changes in the nervous system happen instantly in order to make use of any spare glucose (sugar) in your system to direct energy to the muscles. This results in a dry mouth. Your digestive process has slowed down or stopped as it was using energy that is better served in getting you out of danger. Your body will urge you to get rid of any waste products from your bladder or bowel.

This is the flight response and it saves lives.

The fight response is similar in that you need additional strength and energy to fight off danger. You will probably have experienced a fight response if someone has played a joke and leapt on you from behind. When that happens, people often feel a rush of intense and sudden anger, which is followed by the same sensations described above.

Look again at the sensations of the fight and flight response:
- Breathless
- Shaky
- Dry mouth
- Sweaty

- Needing the toilet
- Tearful
- Frightened
- Nausea or butterflies in the stomach
- Pale face.

Most people describe these same sensations when they talk about anxiety, and many people make the natural assumption that their problem is physical rather than psychological. This is understandable as the sensations are very physical.

What is an Anxiety Disorder?

1 in 10 in Scotland or more

An anxiety disorder differs from normal anxiety in the following ways:
- It is more severe
- It is long-lasting
- It interferes with the person's work or relationships.

Many people with an anxiety disorder do not realise that there are treatments that can help them enjoy a better life. Although up to 1 in 10 Scottish adults have an anxiety disorder, not all will seek professional help.[38]

The National Institute for Clinical Excellence (NICE) Guidelines for Anxiety state the following key points. Anxiety disorders are:
- Common
- Chronic
- The cause of considerable distress and disability
- Often unrecognised and untreated
- Are costly to both the individual and society – if left untreated
- Treatable through a range of effective interventions
- Not permanent. Individuals do get better and remain better
- Improved when people are involved in making decisions about their own treatment and recovery
- Aided by access to information, including support groups.

Anxiety Comes in Different Forms

People can experience anxiety in a general way when they feel worried about many different things for no obvious reason. This is known as **generalised anxiety** and can be very unpleasant. Sometimes people are dismissed as 'just worriers', when in fact they have may have a real mental health problem that can be helped with the right treatment.

General symptoms of anxiety

Anxiety can manifest itself in a variety of ways – physical, psychological and behavioural.

Physical effects:

- Rapid or uneven heartbeat, chest pain, flushing
- Over-breathing, shortness of breath
- Dizziness, headache, sweating, tingling and numbness
- Choking, dry mouth, nausea, vomiting, diarrhoea
- Muscle aches and pains (especially neck, shoulders and lower back), restlessness, tremors and shaking.

Psychological effects:

- Unrealistic or excessive fear and worry (about past or future events)
- Mind racing or going blank
- Decreased concentration and memory
- Difficulty making decisions
- Irritability, impatience, anger
- Confusion
- Restlessness or feeling on edge, nervousness
- Tiredness, sleep disturbances, vivid dreams.

Behavioural effects:

- Avoidance of situations
- Obsessive or compulsive behaviour
- Distress in social situations
- Phobic behaviour.

Other forms of anxiety include **phobias** when certain things or situations bring on an acute anxiety reaction. There are a number of different phobias ranging from social phobia when a person finds it impossible to take part in any social situations, to phobias about specific things such as snakes, spiders or heights.

Post-traumatic stress disorder (PTSD) is a particular form of anxiety brought on by witnessing or being involved in a very traumatic or stressful event. It is normal after such an event to feel distressed and anxious for a few weeks, but PTSD is a long- term reaction that can make it impossible for a person to get on with their lives. In PTSD people commonly have flashbacks in which they have unwelcome memories of the event or feel that they are reliving it.

Panic attacks are very common, and are easily helped by simple first aid methods. A person who has repeated panic attacks, and finds life increasingly difficult to cope with because of the attacks, is said to have **panic disorder**. A phobia that is associated with panic attacks is agoraphobia.

Agoraphobia is not a fear of open spaces – it is anxiety in busy or crowded places. Sometimes this is experienced as a fear of having a panic attack in particular places, especially when the person has already had a panic attack in a similar setting in the past. Sometimes, the fear gets so bad that the person cannot leave his or her own home.

Each of the above forms of anxiety is slightly different, but the thing they all have in common is the unpleasant sensations of anxiety listed opposite. Many people who develop an anxiety disorder find it impossible to believe that the problem is not a physical illness because the sensations are often so manifestly physical.

A mental health first-aider may need to be patient with a person who cannot accept that their problem is anxiety. Your role is not to diagnose or to offer therapy, but to offer comfort when the person is distressed. The techniques in SMHFA work just as well whether or not the person recognises that they are suffering from anxiety.

Mixed Anxiety and Depression

It is very common for people to have both anxiety and depression. Sometimes a person develops one of the disorders first and then the other follows, while in other cases, the two develop at the same time. Often depression occurs when a person has been experiencing anxiety for a long time. This is because managing a high level of anxiety is very distressing and exhausting.

'I couldn't stop thinking about things. They went round and round in my head. After a bit I thought people were avoiding me and I didn't want to go out or socialise with anyone. Eventually I went to my GP because I felt really ill, and she told me it was anxiety.'

Library photo, posed by model.

Specific First Aid for Different Forms of Anxiety

Panic Attacks

Panic attacks are very common – about 1 in 10 people will have one occasionally. A panic attack is a sudden onset of intense apprehension, fear or terror. These attacks can begin suddenly and develop rapidly. This intense fear is not appropriate for the circumstances in which it is happening.

The person experiencing a panic attack often has a sense of impending doom or death. Many of the symptoms are physical ones such as dizziness, shaking, feeling sweaty, nausea, hyperventilating and rapid heartbeat. Many of the physical symptoms can appear similar to those of a heart attack.

Once a person has one of these attacks, they often fear another attack and may avoid places where attacks have occurred. People may also avoid exercise or other activities that can produce physical sensations similar to those of a panic attack.

Some medical conditions have symptoms similar to panic attacks. It is therefore important for the person to have a medical assessment to determine whether they are experiencing a panic attack or have a physical ailment.

How to help a person having a panic attack

If you are in any doubt about whether the person is having a panic attack, a heart attack or an asthma attack, or the person is very distressed, dial 999 and ask for an ambulance. You can get a bystander to do this while you move on to the next step.

- Help to calm the person by encouraging slow, relaxed breathing in unison with your own. You can help the person by gently raising your hand as you say 'breathe in', pause briefly at the top of the breath and then lower your hand as you say 'breathe out'. Each breath should last about three or four seconds and the outwards breath should be as full as possible.

Symptoms
of a panic attack

A person having a panic attack will have several of the following symptoms:

- Increased awareness of heartbeat
- Sweating
- Trembling or shaking
- Feeling of choking, shortness of breath or smothering
- Chest pain or discomfort
- Nausea or abdominal distress
- Feeling of unreality or detachment from oneself or one's surroundings
- Feeling dizzy, unsteady, light-headed or faint
- Fear of losing control or going crazy
- Fear of dying
- Numbness, tingling or pins and needles
- Chills or hot flushes.

- Speak in a slow, calm and gentle way reassuring the person that you know what to do and that they will feel better soon.
- Be a good listener, without judging.
- Explain that the attack will stop soon, and that they will recover fully.
- Assure the person that you will stay with them and keep them safe until the attack stops.

Even if a person is having a heart attack or an asthma attack, you cannot do any harm by following these steps. In fact, the person is likely to benefit as you are helping them to get the most benefit possible from the oxygen they are breathing in.

Phobic Disorders

A person with a phobia avoids or restricts activities because of fear or anxiety. This fear appears persistent, excessive and unreasonable.

They may have an unreasonably strong fear of specific places or events and often avoid these situations completely. Commonly feared situations include leaving home, crowds or public places, speaking in public, travelling in buses, trains or planes, and social events. Others include unexpected things such as buttons or woollen jerseys.

How to help a person with a phobia
We are often unaware that someone has a phobia until we witness his or her response to the situation or the thing they are phobic about. A reaction to a phobia can be very similar to a panic attack as the person reacts with extreme fear.

You can help by:
- Reassuring the person that you are there for them
- Remove the source of the phobia, or take the person away from it
- Listen without judgment
- If the person's breathing is affected, go through the steps above for helping during a panic attack.

Obsessive Compulsive Disorder (OCD)

Obsessive compulsive disorder is relatively common, with approximately 1 or 2 in every 100 people experiencing symptoms. Obsessive thoughts and compulsive behaviours accompany feelings of anxiety. Often the person feels that the only way to control feelings of severe anxiety is to perform certain behaviours or rituals.

Obsessive thoughts are thoughts, images, impulses or ideas that the person cannot get rid of. These thoughts are unwanted and not appropriate to the situation, and cause feelings of acute anxiety. Most obsessive thoughts are about the fear of contamination or harm. The harm can be physical or emotional, so that the person becomes very anxious about things they have said or done, or may possibly say or do in the future.

Compulsive behaviours are repetitive behaviours or mental acts. These may include repeated handwashing, safety checking or silent counting or repeating certain words. The person feels driven to do these things in order to reduce anxiety about an obsession. OCD often begins in adolescence and can return throughout life.

How to help a person with OCD

You can help support a person with obsessive and compulsive disorder by:

- Accepting their feelings as real for them
- Listening if they wish to talk about their symptoms
- Encouraging them to make an appointment with their GP
- Drawing their attention to OCD support groups.

It is worth noting that the family of a person with OCD may benefit from support and a listening ear. Many families report that living with OCD is very stressful.

'The single most helpful thing anyone did for me was to accept my feelings as being real for me. Other people told me I didn't really have anything to worry about, but that was useless to me – it didn't stop me worrying. Instead, it just told me that I shouldn't tell them about it.'

Library photo, posed by model.

Post-traumatic Stress Disorder (PTSD)

Post-traumatic stress disorder occurs after a distressing or catastrophic event. This event may involve actual or threatened death or serious injury. Alternatively, it may involve witnessing such an event. In other cases, learning that such an event has happened to a family member or close friend may also act as a catalyst.

In most cases, the person gets over the event within a month. In instances involving PTSD, the distress lasts longer.

People are more likely to develop PTSD if their response to the traumatic event involves intense fear, helplessness or horror.

In a recent study of asylum seekers, it was found that 79% of those interviewed had witnessed traumatic events such as killings, or had been subject to torture or imprisonment. Of these, almost half were suffering from PTSD.[39]

Symptoms of PTSD:

- Re-experiencing the trauma (recurrent dreams of the event, flashbacks and intrusive memories)
- Unrest in situations that bring back memories of the trauma
- Avoidance behaviour (such as persistent avoidance of things associated with the event)
- Emotional numbing (this may continue for months or years)
- Reduced interest in others and the outside world
- Persistently feeling on edge (constant watchfulness, irritability, jumpiness or being easily startled, outbursts of rage, insomnia).

How to help a person experiencing PTSD
A person with PTSD needs specialist therapy to help deal with the unpleasant symptoms described above.

In the short term, the mental health first-aider can:

- Allow the person to talk about the event or the feelings surrounding the event if they so wish
- Accept that they may need to tell the story several times
- Offer to stay with them if they are feeling very upset or agitated
- Offer kindness and acceptance of the person's experience
- Encourage them to make an appointment with their GP.

You can read more about PTSD at the Royal College of Psychiatrist's website **www.rcpsych.ac.uk/mentalhealthinformation.aspx**

Other reasons
for symptoms of anxiety

Anxiety symptoms can also result from:

- Some medical conditions (overactive thyroid, vitamin B12 deficiency, seizures and some heart conditions)
- The side effects of certain prescription drugs
- Certain non-prescription drugs (caffeine, amphetamines, cocaine, cannabis, ecstasy and LSD).

For these reasons, a person with symptoms of anxiety should always visit their GP for a full medical check.

Some people develop ways of reducing their anxiety that cause further problems. For example, people with phobias avoid anxiety provoking situations. This avoidance reduces their anxiety in the short term but can limit their lives in important ways. Similarly, people with compulsions reduce their anxiety by carrying out repetitive acts such as checking or washing hands. The compulsions then become problems in themselves.

Alcohol and anxiety disorders

Although alcohol can act quickly to relieve feelings of anxiety, long-term alcohol misuse and acute alcohol withdrawal often increases anxiety levels.[40] This can lead people into a destructive cycle of increased alcohol use.

The after-effects of heavy and repeated alcohol use also make everyday living and tasks more difficult to deal with. This leads to additional stress, which in turn can cause or contribute to anxiety.

Caffeine and anxiety disorders

Caffeine gives us a boost and increases feelings of alertness. In higher doses it produces effects similar to anxiety, disrupts sleep and can make panic attacks more likely. People who experience anxious states should reduce their daily intake to 300 mg or less (see opposite). Many people find it best to avoid caffeine altogether.

Illegal drugs and anxiety disorders

Stimulants
Stimulants such as cocaine and amphetamines cause symptoms of anxiety and can induce panic attacks.[41] Cocaine and amphetamines are powerful drugs and should be avoided by people with anxiety. Regular use of ecstasy has also been shown to cause anxiety.[42]

Cannabis and other hallucinogens
Although many people use cannabis to 'chill out', because it intensifies a person's mood it can also worsen the symptoms of anxiety. Cannabis can also cause feelings of anxiety and paranoia and lead to panic attacks. Use of other, more powerful hallucinogens (e.g. LSD or 'magic mushrooms') is also likely to lead to increased anxiety or panic in those with anxiety disorders.

Opiates and other depressant drugs
Some people try to self-medicate with opiates (e.g. heroin) or by misusing prescription drugs such as diazepam (formerly Valium) or nitrazepam (Mogadon). Although these act to relieve feelings of anxiety and worry, all of these drugs are addictive. When taken to combat symptoms of anxiety, they can be even more habit forming. In addition, symptoms usually return as soon as people stop taking them.

It is for the same reasons that drug treatment of anxiety disorders is now less favoured than treatment with counselling techniques.

The caffeine content of some common foods and beverages

Product	Caffeine content (mg)
Coffee	
Instant, weak, 1 level teaspoon	45
Instant, strong, 1 heaped teaspoon	90
Brewed, percolated, 200 ml	100
Filtered, 200 ml	140
Espresso (short black), 100 ml	80
Cappuccino	80
Tea	
Bag or brewed, weak, 200 ml	20
Bag or brewed, strong, 200 ml	70
Soft drinks	
Coke, 375 ml	50
Pepsi, 375 ml	38
Red Bull energy drink	80
Red Eye Platinum	65
Chocolate	
Dark, 50 g	33
Milk, 50 g	12

Modified from *The Choice Health Reader*, Jan/Feb 2001.

What Works for Anxiety

Anxiety can be helped in two ways:

- By learning immediate anxiety-reducing skills so that the person can cope in the short term
- By having longer term treatment that will stop or reduce the onset of anxiety.

Treatments for Anxiety (NICE Guidelines)

When a person begins treatment for anxiety the doctor will:

- Make a careful initial diagnosis based on the person's symptoms
- Check for symptoms of depression, in case the person has mixed anxiety and depression
- Ask about any self-medication the person may have been trying
- Check for possible alcohol problems
- Discuss different treatments that may include:
  - Psychological therapies, such as CBT
  - Medication for short-term treatment
  - Self-help therapies.

Drug treatments
A prescription of anti-anxiety medication may be made in the short term. Antidepressants may be offered for mixed anxiety and depression, and occasionally if panic attacks are frequent and severe.

Psychological treatments
Anxiety disorders are better treated with counselling or psychological techniques than with medication. Such treatments are effective in the short term and continue to be effective long after the actual course of treatment has stopped.

Different methods are used by counsellors and psychotherapists for different forms of anxiety. A good therapist will know what the best approach will be for the individual concerned.

CBT has been found to be very helpful for anxiety because it addresses the thoughts that bring on the feelings and symptoms of anxiety. CBT self-help books and websites can be as helpful for some people as seeing a therapist.

Self-help Treatments for Anxiety

A simple three-point plan for reducing anxiety is:

- Face your fear
- Take more exercise
- Reduce or stop the use of alcohol.

The STEPS team in Glasgow has developed **Eight Quick Control Skills** for helping anxiety in the short term.

1. Mantras
Sit alone in a quiet, dark room. Try to clear your mind as much as possible. Think of a word or phrase, such as:

- 'I am calm'
- 'Relax'
- 'I am in control'.

Close your eyes. Slowly repeat the word or phrase in your mind, over and over. Do this for ten minutes each day or when you feel anxious. If unwanted thoughts come into your mind, try to push them away.

2. Describe your setting
As soon as you feel your stress rise, describe (aloud if you want to) something you can see in great detail, for example,

'I can see a picture on the wall. It is in a dark wood frame. There is a boat on a loch. There is a mountain at the back of the loch. There are trees at the front of the loch. The sky is clear and it looks like it is sunset.'

If you are outside, you can focus on all the sounds you can hear. You should do this in as much detail as you can, as this will help push stressed thoughts out of your mind.

3. 'Worry time'
Put aside 15 minutes each evening. This is your time to worry about the things that have bothered you in the day. Therefore, if you start to worry in the morning, you stop and tell yourself to store it up for your 'worry time' that night. At the start of your 'worry time', think of what you have to worry about and then try to do so. Chances are you may not recall what it was. You may feel it is not worth the worry. Even if you do, you may find it hard to bring on any worry.

4. So, what happened?
Carry a note pad with you. Write down the things you worry about and rate the chances of them happening, e.g. 100% means it will happen, 60% means it might happen, and so on. Look through your diary a few days later and see if they did happen. Keep doing this. You might find that you can stop the worry more easily as you stand back and rate the chances.

5. Coping with a tension headache

Try this if you feel a tight band round the front and back of your scalp. Change your posture – do not sit all hunched up. Get some support for the small of your back. Find the groove in the back of your neck. Curl up the fingers of both hands. Push them into the groove as hard as you can. Tilt your head back at the same time. Hold this for about one minute. Repeat this as often as you need to.

6. One goal a day

Try this if you feel you do not have a good structure to the day or if you do not get round to doing things. Each night, work out a goal for the next day. This should be something you are not doing but should be doing. It might be something like:

- Get up with the family
- Cut the grass
- Vacuum the hall
- Meet a friend at the shops
- Fill out a form.

In other words, the usual things you would do if you felt on top of things. Try to make your goals precise, such as 'cut the grass' not 'do a bit in the garden'. This helps you know whether you have achieved what you set out to achieve. If the grass is cut or the hall vacuumed, then you have achieved your goal and a pat on the back is in order. The aim is for you to go to bed each night and be able to say to yourself that you have taken at least one step forward. This will build you up for your next goal.

7. Breathing retraining

This is a quick way to calm your body. It can also help prevent panic.

- Sit in a comfy chair and relax as much as you can.
- Take a slow normal breath (not a deep breath) and think 'one' to yourself.
- As you breathe out, think 'relax'.
- Breathe in again and think 'two'.
- Breathe out and think 'relax'.
- Keep doing this up to ten.
- When you reach ten, reverse and start back down to one.
- Try to put all else out of your mind.
- Try to see the numbers and the word 'relax' in your mind's eye.

Do not be put off if you cannot do this straight away. You can boost the benefits of this by using Quick Control Skill 8.

8. Breathing from the diaphragm

Place one hand on your chest and the other over your belly button. As you breathe in, the hand on your stomach should be pushed out while the hand on your chest should not move. As you breathe out, your stomach should pull in. Your chest should not move.

To help, breathe in through your nose, then purse your lips and breathe out slowly through your mouth. If you are a chest breather, you may find this hard at first. If you cannot get the hang of this, lie on your back on the floor and practise. You will find this easier.

Put these two breathing exercises (skills 7 and 8) together and do them twice a day. Once you get good at them, do them when you are at work, sitting on the bus, watching TV etc. The aim is to be able to do this no matter where you are. No one will notice you doing them.

Continuing Treatment for Anxiety

The stepped-care approach to treatment for anxiety involves offering regular reviews to the person with anxiety so that treatment can be changed as necessary.

Follow-up appointments will be offered to the person and she or he will be given information about alternative treatments where appropriate. Where treatments by the local health care team prove to be unsuccessful, the person will be referred to specialist mental health services.

'I wish somebody had sat down with me years ago and told me – you don't have to be like this. I didn't know other people had been through it too.'

Library photo, posed by model.

First Aid for **Anxiety**

Ask about suicide

Listen non-judgmentally

Give reassurance and information

Encourage the person to get appropriate help

Encourage self-help strategies

Ask about suicide

A person who has been experiencing a high level of anxiety for a long time can become very depressed and feel that living life with these feelings is too difficult. Be aware that the person may be having suicidal thoughts and ask the question where appropriate. Remember to refer back to the section on Suicide, on page 38.

Listen non-judgmentally

People who are very anxious may be sensitive to criticism or judgment. As a mental health first-aider, you can offer kindness and non-judgmental support by listening to their concerns.

How to listen to an anxious person:

- Accept the person's worries or fears as real for them
- Do not try to reason with them or persuade them that they are worrying unnecessarily
- Do not go into 'problem-solving mode'
- Encourage the person to talk about how they feel as well as the thing they are anxious about
- Offer the simple comfort of 'being there' for the person.

Disagreeing with a person's worries does not help them feel better. Accept what they are saying without judgment, and tell the person that feeling the way they do must be unpleasant.

step 3

Give reassurance and information

Once you have listened to the person and allowed them space to tell you of their anxiety, you can offer reassurance by telling the person that:

- An anxiety disorder is a common illness
- An anxiety disorder is not a weakness or a character defect
- Effective help is available
- Skills can be learned to reduce the effects of stress and anxiety
- Anxiety can be unpleasant but is rarely harmful.

step 4

Encourage the person to get professional help

Encourage the person to see a GP first. An understanding GP will provide:

- A full physical check to ensure that there is no physical condition causing the symptoms
- Education about the nature of the anxiety disorder
- Ongoing appointments for counselling and support
- Referral to a clinical psychologist or a mental health worker who can provide cognitive behaviour therapy.

step 5

Encourage self-help strategies

In the short term there are a number of very effective ways of easing immediate feelings of anxiety. These include taking exercise, avoiding caffeine, learning relaxation techniques and talking to a trusted person. Read more about what works for anxiety on page 100.

Organisations

Action on Depression
www.actionondepression.org
Provides information and support to
people with depression and their carers,
and also lists details of local self-help
groups.

**British Association for Behavioural
and Cognitive Therapists**
www.babcp.com
Tel: 0161 705 4304

Nationwide listings of psychotherapists.

**British Association for Counselling
and Psychotherapy**
www.bacp.co.uk
Tel: 0145 588 3300

Nationwide listings of counsellors and
psychotherapists.

The British Psychological Society
www.bps.org.uk
Tel: 0116 254 9568

Nationwide listings of counsellors and
psychotherapists.

Anxiety UK
www.anxietyuk.org.uk
Tel: 08444 775 774

Support and help for those diagnosed
with, or who suspect that they have an
anxiety disorder. Also, help dealing with
specific phobias. Online support by email
is available through the website.

No Panic
www.nopanic.org.uk
Tel: 0844 967 4848

Aids the relief and rehabilitation of
people who experience anxiety disorders,
and supports their families and carers.
Help and information is also offered
for anxiety-related issues, including
tranquilliser withdrawal.

Know the Score
www.knowthescore.info
Tel: 0800 587 5879

A free and confidential drugs information
and advice line.

Combat Stress
www.combatstress.org.uk

Combat Stress is the UK's veterans'
mental health charity.

Living Life to the Full
www.llttf.com

A Scottish interactive site for depression
and anxiety, where users can access
cognitive behaviour therapy (CBT)
treatments online.

Self- Help Books

Williams, C. (2003). *Overcoming
Anxiety:* **A Five Areas Approach.
Arnold: London.**
A self-help book based on cognitive
behaviour therapy (CBT).

Bourne, E. (1995). *The Anxiety and
Phobia Workbook.* **New Harbinger
Publications: Oakland, CA.**
A self-help book based on cognitive
behaviour therapy (CBT).

Marks, I. (2001). *Living with Fear.* McGraw-Hill Education, Maidenhead: UK.

This book, based on cognitive behaviour therapy (CBT), includes a very useful chapter on self-help for fears and anxiety. Research has shown that people with phobias who follow the instructions in this chapter improve as much as people treated by a professional.

Rapee, R.M. (1998). *Overcoming Shyness and Social Phobia.* Lifestyle Press: Killara NSW.

This book teaches how to overcome social phobia using cognitive behaviour therapy (CBT).

Additional Reading

Talking about Anxiety Disorders.
Part of the 'Talking About' series of leaflets. www.healthscotland.com/documents/1002.aspx
Edinburgh: NHS Health Scotland, 2015
ISBN 978-1-84485-320-5

Talking about Panic Attacks.
Part of the 'Talking About' series of leaflets.
www.healthscotland.com/documents/2186.aspx
Edinburgh: NHS Health Scotland, 2015
ISBN 1-84485-305-5

Talking about Phobias
Part of the'Talking About' series of leaflets.
www.healthscotland.com/documents/2185.aspx
Edinburgh: NHS Health Scotland, 2015
ISBN 978-1-84485-384-7

Psychosis

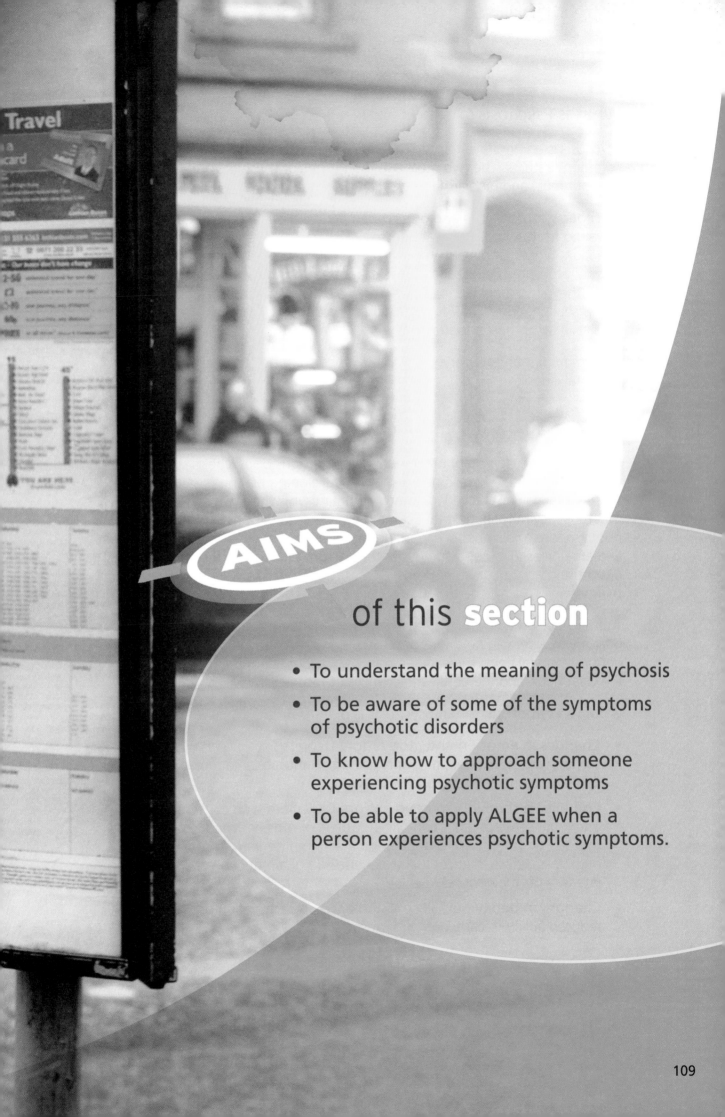

of this **section**

- To understand the meaning of psychosis

- To be aware of some of the symptoms of psychotic disorders

- To know how to approach someone experiencing psychotic symptoms

- To be able to apply ALGEE when a person experiences psychotic symptoms.

What is Psychosis?

Psychosis is an umbrella term for a range of disorders that share some common features. The two most common forms of psychosis are schizophrenia and bipolar disorder (manic depression).

Psychotic symptoms can also occur when people are in Intensive Care Units suffering from serious physical illnesses; in elderly people with an acute infection; when people have brain damage; and in people with drug and alcohol problems. People sometimes experience psychotic-like symptoms when they are exhausted, or after a serious shock. The guidance provided in this section, about how to approach a person with psychotic symptoms, applies in all of these situations.

Bear in mind that not everyone who is experiencing psychotic symptoms has a mental illness.

How do I Know if Someone is Experiencing Psychosis?

It is important to learn about the early warning signs of psychosis so that you can recognise when someone may be developing psychosis. Although these signs may not be very dramatic on their own, when you consider them together they may suggest that something is not quite right. It is important not to ignore or dismiss such warning signs – even if they appear gradually and are unclear. Do not assume that the person is just going through a phase or misusing alcohol or other drugs, or that the symptoms will go away on their own.

The only person who can diagnose psychosis is a psychiatrist, but a mental health first-aider can be aware of the signs and can encourage a person to get professional help. The earlier a psychosis is identified, the more effective the treatment, and the better the chances of recovery.

Common symptoms when psychosis is developing: [43]

- **Changes in emotion and motivation:** Depression; anxiety; irritability; suspiciousness; blunted, flat, unexpected or unusual emotion; change in appetite; reduced energy and motivation.

- **Changes in thinking and perception:** Difficulties with concentration or attention; sense of alteration of self, others or outside world (e.g. feeling that self or others have changed or are acting differently in some way); odd ideas; unusual perceptual experiences (e.g. a reduction or greater intensity of smell, sound or colour).

- **Changes in behaviour:** Sleep disturbance; social isolation or withdrawal; reduced ability to carry out work or social roles.

Common symptoms when psychosis has developed: [44]

- **Unusual experiences:** The most common unusual experience associated with psychosis involves hearing voices. However, unusual experiences can also involve seeing, feeling, tasting and smelling things that are not there. During the early stages of psychosis, individuals are often frightened by the voices they hear because they might believe that 'I am going mad'. Later, voices can be frightening because the person feels that they have no control over them, or that the voices are too powerful. These voices may encourage the person to act in a way that they do not want to.

- **Unusual Beliefs:** Unusual beliefs or delusions commonly occur in psychosis. The most common type of unusual beliefs are 'delusions of persecution' or paranoid beliefs – these occur when people believe that someone is deliberately trying to harm them. Another common set of beliefs are 'ideas of reference', in which people worry that other people, the television or radio, magazines or newspapers are talking about them. 'Delusions of control', where people believe that their actions are being controlled by someone or something else (such as God, the Devil, aliens or other people) are also common. Other common unusual beliefs include thinking that one's thoughts are being broadcast, believing that thoughts are being put in one's head, and thinking that one has been chosen for a task or is very special in some way. Finally, 'grandiose delusions' involve very inflated self-esteem in which the person may believe that he or she is superhuman, especially talented or an important religious figure.

The signs or symptoms of psychosis vary from person to person and can change over time. We should always bear in mind that what is considered normal in one culture might be interpreted as a symptom of psychosis in another culture.

Types of Mental Health Problems Associated with Psychosis

It is important to remember that not all individuals who have psychotic experiences have a mental illness. Psychotic experiences such as hearing voices and suspiciousness or paranoia occur in the general population, and to some extent are normal and understandable responses to stressful life events. Some reactions to drugs and alcohol are very similar to psychotic episodes. Equally, it is important not to minimise a person's experience of psychosis, especially when the person asks for help, is emotionally distressed or experiencing changes in their behaviour that make it difficult to function in their usual way.

A person with psychotic symptoms may eventually be diagnosed with schizophrenia.

Schizophrenia

Schizophrenia has nothing to do with 'split personality'. The term schizophrenia means 'fractured mind' and refers to changes in mental function whereby thoughts and perceptions are altered.

About 1% of people develop schizophrenia at some stage in their lives. Nearly three-quarters of them are first affected when they are between the ages of 16 and 25. Schizophrenia affects males and females equally, but males tend to develop it earlier than females. The onset of the illness may be rapid, with symptoms developing over several weeks, or it may be slow and develop over months or years. At any given time, a person with a diagnosis of schizophrenia may be experiencing severe symptoms, mild symptoms or none at all.

The early stages of schizophrenia are often missed because the person behaves like a typical adolescent. Boys often have their first symptoms of psychosis around the age of 16 to 18. These symptoms might include:

- Withdrawing from others or spending a lot of time alone

- Lack of interest in personal hygiene

- Suspiciousness

- Moodiness

- Blunted emotion.

How should I approach someone
who may be experiencing psychotic symptoms?

People developing a psychotic disorder will often not reach out for help. Someone who is experiencing profound and frightening changes such as psychotic symptoms will often try to keep them a secret. If you are worried about someone, approach the person in a caring and non-judgmental manner to discuss your concerns. The person you are trying to help might not trust you, or they might be afraid of being perceived as 'different' or as 'mad', and therefore may not be open with you. They may be frightened of being hospitalised or being seen as a 'schizophrenic'. On the other hand, they may feel embarrassed and ashamed of the associated stigma of mental illness. If possible, you should approach the person privately about their experiences, in a place that is free of distractions.

Try to tailor your approach to suit the way the person is behaving (e.g. if the person is suspicious and is avoiding eye contact, be sensitive to this and give them the space they need). Do not touch the person without their permission. You should state the specific behaviours you are concerned about, and you should not speculate about the person's diagnosis.

It is easy to understand why these symptoms are often missed. The diagnosis of schizophrenia can take up to two years because it is common for people to have a single episode of psychosis and then completely recover. A diagnosis will only be made once the psychiatrist is certain that this is more than a single episode.

Bipolar Disorder (manic depression)

A person with bipolar disorder experiences bouts of severe depression, which might be so serious that the person's life is at risk. At other times, they also experience bouts of mania. Another name for this is manic depressive disorder. Bipolar disorder is covered in this section because there are times when the person has a different sense of reality to other people. They may hear or see things that others do not, and they may also think very differently to other people. This causes the person to make decisions and act in ways that are out of character and are sometimes risky.

Mania is the opposite of depression. A person experiencing mania may:

- Be overconfident and full of energy
- Be very talkative
- Find it difficult to stick to one subject in conversation
- Be full of ideas
- Have less need for sleep
- Take unusual and dangerous risks

It is important to allow the person to talk about their experiences and beliefs if they want to. As far as possible, let the person set the pace and style of the conversation. You should recognise that they might be frightened by their thoughts and feelings. Ask the person about what will help them to feel safe and in control.

Reassure them that you are there to help and support them, and that you want to keep them safe. If possible, offer the person choices of how you can help them so that they are in control. Assure them that help is available and that things can get better.

If the person is unwilling to talk with you, do not try to force them to talk about their experiences. Rather, let them know that you will be available if they would like to talk in the future. The majority of people who have psychotic symptoms are not a risk to other people, but they may be very frightened by the symptoms they are experiencing.

People with mental illnesses are far more often victims of crime and violence. However, occasionally a frightened person will lash out if they feel threatened. Keeping yourself and the person safe is a priority.

- Become unclear about what is real
- Be over active to the point that their physical health is at risk
- Over spend to an extent that their financial security is seriously threatened.

Although mania may sound like fun, it often gets people into difficult situations and they may take risks, or become exhausted and very distressed. Correct diagnosis of bipolar disorder can take a long time. This is because the person needs to have had episodes of both depression and mania. Different people take different amounts of time to move between these two extremes (sometimes years).

Drug-induced psychosis is a form of psychosis brought on by the use of illegal or recreational drugs. The symptoms usually appear quickly and last a short time (from a few hours to days) until the effects of the drug wears off. Although drugs can sometimes be the sole cause of psychosis, in other cases they may trigger another psychotic illness, such as schizophrenia, in people who are vulnerable to psychosis. [45]

Alcohol-induced psychosis normally passes when the person has recovered from the effects of alcohol misuse, but it is not clear whether it can also cause a more enduring psychosis. Alcohol interferes with some anti-psychotic medications.

How Can I be Supportive?

Treat the person with respect. You should try to empathise with how the person feels regarding their beliefs and experiences. Do not make judgments about the content of those beliefs and experiences. The person may be behaving and talking differently due to psychotic symptoms. They may also find it difficult to tell what is real from what is not real.

You should avoid confronting the person and should not criticise or blame them. Understand the symptoms for what they are and try not to take them personally. Do not use sarcasm and try to avoid patronising statements.

It is important that you are honest when interacting with the person. Do not make any promises that you cannot keep.

'Schizophrenia is a really scary thing to face, but it's much more scary not to face it.'

Library photo, posed by model.

How Do I Deal with Delusions and Hallucination?

It is important to recognise that the delusions (false beliefs) and hallucinations (perceiving things that are not real) are very real to the person. You should not dismiss, minimise or argue with the person about their delusions or hallucinations. Similarly, do not act alarmed, horrified or embarrassed. You should not laugh at the person's symptoms of psychosis. If the person exhibits paranoid behaviour, remain calm and do not encourage or inflame the person's paranoia.

How Do I Deal with Communication Difficulties?

People experiencing symptoms of psychosis are often unable to think clearly. You should respond to disorganised speech by communicating in an uncomplicated and straightforward manner. Repeat things if necessary. After you say something, you should be patient and allow plenty of time for the person to process the information and respond. If the person is showing a limited range of feelings, you should be aware that it does not mean that the person is not feeling anything. Likewise, you should not assume the person cannot understand what you are saying, even if their response is limited.

First Aid for **Psychosis**

Ask about suicide

Listen non-judgmentally

Give reassurance and information

Encourage the person to get appropriate help

Encourage self-help strategies

step 1

Ask about suicide

People with psychosis are at a high risk of suicide or self-harm. The Royal College of Psychiatrists estimates that 1 in 10 people with a psychosis die by suicide.[46] (See the Suicide section on page 38 if you are at all concerned that the person is at risk.) There is also the possibility that the person may believe that they are at risk of harm from others, which can make it difficult to offer reassurance.

If the person is very distressed, it might be more appropriate to watch and listen carefully to the person rather than ask the question about suicide. Remain as calm as possible and think about the risks involved (e.g. whether there is any risk that the person will harm themselves or others). Try to find out if the person has anyone she or he trusts (e.g. close friends, family) and try to enlist their help. If the person is very distressed, it is best that someone stays with them.

If you are in any doubt about whether the person is a risk to him or herself, you should call for immediate help.

It is important to:

- Communicate to the person in a clear and concise manner and use short, simple sentences
- Speak quietly in a non-threatening tone of voice at a moderate pace
- Calmly answer any questions that the person may ask
- Comply with requests, unless they are unsafe or unreasonable. This gives the person the opportunity to feel some control
- Always tell the person clearly what is going on, e.g. 'Here is an ambulance. They are coming to help.'

You should be aware that the person might act upon a delusion or hallucination. Remember that your primary task is to give first aid and therefore you should not do anything to agitate the person further. Try to maintain safety by protecting the person, yourself and others around you from harm. Make sure that you have access to an exit.

If the person appears to be at risk of harming themselves or others, you should call for help immediately. Dial 999 and ask for an ambulance. Once the ambulance arrives, explain to the paramedics what you have observed and your concerns. You should explain to the person you are helping who any unfamiliar people are, that they are there to help and how they are going to help.

step 2

Listen non-judgmentally

A person experiencing psychosis is often distressed and very anxious. They may not want to talk to you about how they are feeling, but it is appropriate to offer to listen if it would help.

- Remain calm.
- Do not agree or disagree with statements that seem to be about a delusion.
- You can respond by saying something like, 'I can't hear the voices you are hearing but it sounds as though they are upsetting you.'
- Accept what the person tells you as real for them.
- Show empathy by recognising how distressed they are.
- Offer to call someone the person feels safe with.

What if the person is very agitated?

People with psychosis are not usually aggressive and are at a much higher risk of harming themselves than others. However, certain symptoms of psychosis (e.g. delusions or hallucinations) can cause people to become aggressive. Unfortunately, the media tends to publicise the few people with mental illness who become violent. In fact, people with psychosis are themselves at greater risk from violent crime. A study of people in British inner cities found that 16% of people with psychosis had been the victims of violence. This compares with 7% of the inner city population overall.[47]

You should know how to de-escalate the situation if the person you are trying to help becomes aggressive. Take any threats or warnings seriously, particularly if the person believes they are being persecuted. If you are frightened, seek outside help immediately. You should never put yourself at risk. If you feel unsafe at any time, remove yourself from the situation and dial 999. When help arrives, you should not assume the person is experiencing a psychotic episode, but should clearly state what you have observed and explain what your concerns are.

What to do if someone is very agitated and threatening

1. Ensure your own personal safety – do not physically attempt to stop any violence or to restrain the person, unless in self-defence.

2. Call for help – the person may have a Crisis Card or Advance Statement that may help in identifying who to contact. If there is any threat of serious aggression or violence, call the police. Tell the police you think the person has a mental illness and needs to get medical help. Ask them to send a plain-clothes police officer if possible, so the person will feel less threatened.

3. Try to create a calm, non-threatening atmosphere, talk slowly, quietly, firmly and simply. Keep the environment free from distractions (e.g. turn off the television or radio). Do not get too close to the person. Many people with psychosis need more personal space than usual. Keep at a reasonable distance, avoid continuous eye contact and do not touch the person.

4. Try to get the person to sit down. When people are seated, they may feel more at ease. It is best you are both seated side-by-side rather than face-to-face. If the person sits down and you remain standing the person can feel threatened. If appropriate, give or share something to help create some trust such as food or a non-alcoholic drink.

5. Do not try to reason with someone who may be experiencing acute psychosis. Try not to express irritation or anger. Do not threaten, shout or criticise. Remember that they may be acting in this way because of delusions or voices that are very real and very frightening to them.

6. Express empathy for the person's emotional distress. However, it is very important that you do not pretend that the delusions or voices are real to you.

7. Comply with reasonable requests – this will provide the person with a feeling that they are somewhat in control.

Give reassurance and information

When a person is experiencing psychosis, you should give small amounts of information in a very clear way. Providing reassurance may mean explaining that you will help the person in any way you can, that you will stay with them if they want your support and that you can call someone who will know what to do to make them feel better.

Information may not be what the person needs at this time, but if they ask you about something give an honest and clear reply.

Encourage the person to get professional help

Psychosis is a serious and complex issue and only a psychiatrist can make a diagnosis of a psychotic illness. In the first instance, the person should be encouraged to see their GP.

You should ask the person if they have felt this way before and if so, what they have done in the past that has been helpful. Try to find out what type of assistance they believe will help them.

You should also try to determine whether the person has a supportive social network and if they do, encourage them to use these supports.

If the person decides to seek professional help, they may require help to make sure that they are supported both emotionally and practically to access the services they need. If the person does seek help, and is not happy with the medical advice they have received, they should seek a second opinion from another medical or mental health professional.

It is important to get the person to medical help as early in the development of the illness as possible. Outcomes are better the sooner people get help. A person with a psychotic illness needs to see a doctor.

What if the person does not want help?

The person may refuse to seek help even if they realise they are unwell. Their confusion and fear about what is happening to them may lead them to deny that anything is wrong. In this case, you should encourage them to talk to someone they trust.

It is also possible that a person will refuse to seek help because they lack the insight that they are unwell. They might actively resist your attempts to encourage them to seek help. In either case, your course of action should depend on the type and severity of the person's symptoms.

It is important to recognise that unless a person with psychosis meets the criteria for involuntary treatment, they cannot be forced into treatment. If they are not at risk of harming themselves or others, you should remain patient. People experiencing psychosis often need time to develop insight regarding their illness. Never threaten the person with the Mental Health Act or hospitalisation. Instead, remain friendly and open to the possibility that they may want your help in the future.

In the case of family or close friends, there is no easy solution if a psychotic person is unwilling to seek professional help.

The following may be helpful:

1. Talk to other people who have been in a similar situation, for example at a mental health carers' support group.

2. Make an appointment for yourself with a GP or a mental health professional to talk about the problem.

3. A GP is the first professional to turn to. They can make an initial assessment and diagnosis, prescribe medication, and refer the person to the community mental health team (CMHT) for specialist assessment and advice on medication and treatment.

4. Psychiatrists are medical specialists who treat mental health problems. A GP should refer a person with a suspected psychotic illness to a psychiatrist for diagnosis and expert advice on treatment. A person who is severely psychotic may require a short stay in hospital to stabilise the psychosis.

step 5

Encourage self-help strategies

In a crisis, a person with psychosis may not be able to benefit from self-help, but later in their treatment a number of self-help strategies have been found to help.

A mental health first-aider may be able to offer support to a person in treatment as they try different forms of self-help.

Family and friends can also be a very important source of support for a person with a psychotic illness. A person is more likely to stay well if they have a good relationship with their family.[48]

Helping the family of a person with psychosis

Sometimes the most useful thing a first-aider can do is to support the family of a person with psychosis.

A diagnosis of psychosis has a huge impact on the person's family and can cause all kinds of stress and anxiety.

ALGEE is a very useful approach when supporting a person in this situation.

What helps psychosis?

Early Intervention

Early intervention is very important. However, due to the complexity of the problems and the reluctance to label a person, this is often delayed. The consequences of delayed help include:

- Slower and less complete recovery
- Poorer long-term functioning
- Increased risk of depression and suicide
- Slower maturing psychologically and slower uptake of adult responsibilities
- Strain on relationships with friends and family resulting in loss of social supports
- Disruption of study and employment
- Increased use of alcohol and drugs
- Loss of self-esteem and confidence
- Greater chance of problems with the law.

Psychological Therapies

Cognitive behaviour therapy (CBT) and 'family therapies' have been recognised as being helpful in the treatment of psychosis. These approaches are particularly useful in helping the person cope with distressing psychotic experiences, as well as to reduce the impact of future episodes by highlighting recovery, understanding and planning.

Self-help

- Relaxation methods to reduce tension
- Information
- Regular exercise, sleep and a healthy diet
- Avoiding overly stressful situations
- The use of support groups.

Drug Treatments

Most people with an acute psychotic illness require medication. The use of drug treatments in psychosis can include anti-psychotic medication, mood stabilising medication and antidepressants.

Recovery

People do recover from psychotic illness. The actual percentage of people who recover is difficult to assess as many people have one brief episode and do not go for professional help. For every five people who develop schizophrenia:

- 1 in 5 will get better within five years of their first episode of schizophrenia

- 3 in 5 will get better, but will still have some symptoms. They will have times when their symptoms get worse

- 1 in 5 will continue to have troublesome symptoms.[49]

For a person with bipolar disorder, the chance of repeated episodes of the illness are high, but with the right support and effective medical treatment, a person with bipolar disorder can remain well for a long time.[50]

As with all mental health problems, the things that aid recovery are common to everyone. These include effective support, a secure home, healthy food, exercise and fresh air, enjoyable activities, medication when needed and the knowledge that other people are caring for you.

'It's been good to get to know others who have been through it too. The group was a chance to make new positive relationships.'

Library photo, posed by model.

Organisations

Support in Mind
www.supportinmindscotland.org.uk
Tel: 0131 662 4359
Email: info@supportinmindscotland.org.uk

An educational and support organisation that works to improve the wellbeing and quality of life of those affected by schizophrenia and other mental illness.

Bipolar Scotland
www.bipolarscotland.org.uk
Tel: 0141 560 2050

Works to empower people in Scotland who are in contact with bipolar disorder.

Hearing Voices Network
www.hearing-voices.org
Tel: 0114 271 8210

We offer information, support and understanding to people who hear voices and those who support them.

Scottish Recovery Network
www.scottishrecovery.net
Email: info@scottishrecovery.net

Promotes and supports recovery from long-term mental health problems in Scotland.

MIND
www.mind.org.uk

Works to create a better life for everyone with experience of mental distress.

Rethink
www.rethink.org
Tel: 0121 522 7007
Email: advice@rethink.org

Runs project and support groups for people with severe mental health problems, their carers, friends and families. Call for details about what is available in your area.

Self-help Books

Blackman, L. (2001). *Hearing Voices: contesting the voice of reason.* Free Association Books: London

Provides information on an alternative approach to hearing voices

Additional Reading

Talking About Schizophrenia.

Part of the 'Talking About' series of leaflets.
www.healthscotland.com/documents/1475.aspx
Edinburgh: NHS Health Scotland, 2015
ISBN 978-1-84485-303-8

Talking about Bipolar Affective Disorder.

Part of the 'Talking About' series of leaflets.
www.healthscotland.com/documents/1550.aspx
Edinburgh: NHS Health Scotland, 2015
ISBN 978-1-84485-377-9

Scottish Government's Strategic Objective for Health

'Help people to sustain and improve their health, especially in disadvantaged communities, ensuring better, local and faster access to health care.'
Scottish Government Strategic Objective. www.scotland.gov.uk/About/Performance/scotPerforms/objectives/healthier

Mental Health Strategy for Scotland

'The Scottish Government's mental health strategy to 2015 sets out a range of key commitments across the full spectrum of mental health improvement, services and recovery to ensure delivery of effective, quality care and treatment for people with a mental illness, their carers and families.'
Mental Health Strategy for Scotland: 2012–2015. www.scotland.gov.uk/Publications/2012/08/9714

Seven themes for mental health

Seven key themes emerged from the consultation on the Mental Health Strategy.

1. Working more effectively with families and carers
Families and carers can have an important role in providing support to those with mental illness.

2. Embedding more peer to peer work and support
The work that was taken forward under Delivering for Mental Health to establish paid peer-support workers.

3. Increasing the support for self management and self help approaches
The evidence base for people taking a leading role in managing their own illness over time and the wider benefits to them that this approach offers is well established.

4. Extending the anti-stigma agenda forward to include further work on discrimination
The work that has been taken forward in Scotland through See Me is internationally recognised as establishing best practice and has been drawn on and adopted throughout the world.

5. Focusing on the rights of those with mental illness
The Mental Health (Care and Treatment) (Scotland) Act 2003 established core principles to apply to mental health services in Scotland and has firmly embedded rights at the heart of practice within services.

6. Developing the outcomes approach to include personal, social and clinical outcomes
The Scottish Recovery Network was established in 2004 to take forward the recovery model in Scotland. Recovery is the idea that individuals and services should look beyond purely clinical outcomes to see the whole person and their social and personal outcomes as equally valid.

7. Ensuring that we use new technology effectively as a mechanism for providing and delivering evidence-based services.
Many people already look to the internet and other new media approaches for help when they are in distress and this trend is likely to continue.

Health Improvement in Scotland

The Scottish Government's purpose is to focus the government and public services on creating a more prosperous country, with opportunities for all of Scotland to flourish, through increasing sustainable economic growth.

Five strategic objectives underpin this purpose and describe the kind of Scotland we want to live in – a Scotland that is wealthier and fairer, healthier, safer and stronger, smarter and greener. The government's 'healthier' objective is to:

Help people to sustain and improve their health, especially in disadvantaged communities, ensuring better, local and faster access to health care.

The government aims to help people lead longer, healthier lives. In achieving this goal, the approach should focus on individuals, communities and areas most at risk of poor health outcomes. This means challenging the health inequalities that currently exist in Scotland. This applies equally to both physical and mental health.

Mental Health Policy in Scotland

Mental health policy in Scotland, complemented by modern legislation, covers promotion, prevention, care, treatment and recovery. It is underpinned by a commitment to enhancing social inclusion and tackling health and other inequalities.

Scotland's Mental Health First Aid is an ongoing key initiative that is funded by the Scottish Government and NHS Health Scotland.

It works to support and improve the mental health of people in Scotland, and is part of the government's mental health improvement agenda.

The NHS in Scotland

NHS Scotland promotes the positive message of mental wellbeing and aims to ensure that all people, whether they are experiencing mental ill health or not, receive the same quality service and are treated equally.

Key initiatives influencing and supporting the mental health improvement agenda include:

- **see me** – the national anti-stigma campaign
- **Choose Life** – Scotland's national strategy and action plan for preventing suicide
- **Breathing Space** – an advice line and referral service for people experiencing low mood or depression (this service is particularly targeted at young men)
- **Scotland's Mental Health First Aid**
- **The Scottish Recovery Network**
- **The Scottish Centre for Healthy Working Lives** – a programme for improving mental health in employment and working life.

Information on how to contact the above organisations can be found in the 'Helpful Resources' at the end of each section.

Other associated programmes or resources include:

- *Delivering for Mental Health* www.scotland.gov.uk/ publications/2006/11/30164829/0
- *Better Health, Better Care: Action Plan* www.scotland.gov.uk/ publications/2007/12/ 11103453/0
- Living Life to the Full www.llttf.com
- *Equally Well: Report of the Ministerial Task Force on Health Inequalities* www.scotland.gov.uk/ publications/2008/ 06/25104032/0

There are many ways of explaining the factors that influence our health. Scotland's Mental Health First Aid has chosen to use the Mental Health Continuum as a useful model for showing how factors such as time and circumstances can influence a person's mental health. In other words, there is more to mental health than whether or not a person has a diagnosis of an illness. It is impossible to cover the range of ideas and theories about health in a 12-hour course. We have included a brief description of another popular model to give an overview of one alternative way of considering health.

This model by Dahlgren and Whitehead pays closer attention to the impact of lifestyle, social and economic circumstances, culture and the environment. It attempts to show how these things influence an individual's health and how they interact with one another.

The model shows that health is affected both positively and negatively by a range of different factors, from those specific to the individual, to wider cultural and social issues.

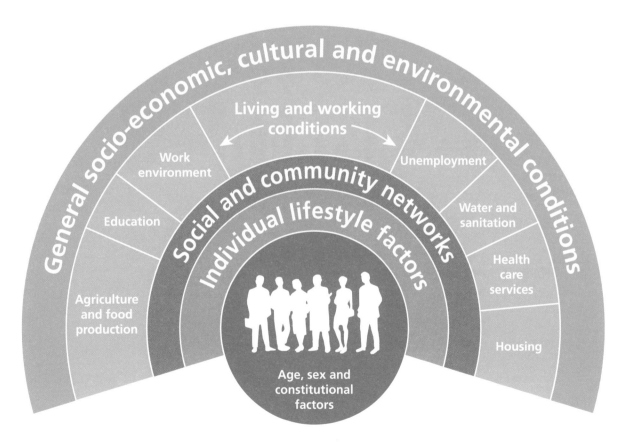

Source: Dahlgren G, Whitehead M. (1991). *Policies and Strategies to Promote Social Equity in Health*. Stockholm, Sweden: Institute for Futures Studies.[51]

An individual's health will be influenced by their gender, age, and by their individual personality and relative strength or resilience. However, health is much more than individual factors. A person's health is affected by their local community and the extent to which they have a sense of belonging. Education, work, the ability to access and prepare healthy food, housing and sanitation are also significant factors, as are economic, cultural and environmental conditions.

This model is useful for considering the extent to which a person has control over their own health, and how much health improvement needs to be driven by policy that recognises the impact of all these factors. The model also acts as an important reminder that health is not purely about the individual.

It is therefore unhelpful and misguided to blame those who are experiencing poor health.

Source: Dahlgren G, Whitehead M. (1991). *Policies and Strategies to Promote Social Equity in Health*. Stockholm, Sweden: Institute for Futures Studies.[51]

Mental Health and Age

As with all groups in society, there is a strong connection between a person's individual life stage or situation and their mental health. Some mental health problems are more common at certain ages. Young people, for instance, are more likely to begin using self-harm as a means of coping with feelings of distress. Schizophrenia is much more likely to emerge in young people between the ages of 16 and 25 than any other age, and young men under the age of 35 are currently at greater risk of suicide than any other group.

Growing older does not mean that a person will inevitably become unwell. However, evidence shows that people over the age of 65 are at much greater risk of becoming depressed than any other age group. 1 in 4 people over the age of 65 has symptoms of depression, and 40% of those in care homes are depressed.[52] Age UK highlights the prevalence of undiagnosed depression in older people. Half of older people with symptoms of depression go undiagnosed by their GPs, and may benefit from help identifying their symptoms and discussing them with a doctor.[53]

While life events such as retirement or physical illness can have an impact on mental health, mental health problems are not an inevitable part of growing older. Evidence from the UK inquiry into Mental Health and Wellbeing in Later Life shows that the five main areas that influence mental health in later life are:

- **Discrimination** and in particular the double disadvantage of age discrimination and discrimination against people with mental health problems

- **Participation** in meaningful activity – staying active and involved can help prevent mental health problems

- **Relationships** that are secure and supportive are important for good mental health and wellbeing

- **Physical health** and mental health are inextricably linked. Good physical health is associated with good mental health

- **Poverty** is a risk factor for poor mental health. It is not money *per se* but the things it can provide that are important to making people feel included in society in later life.[54]

Mental Health and Disability

Mental health problems are considered a disability when there is a significant impact upon a person that lasts for longer than 12 months. This means that a person with a long-standing mental health problem is protected against discrimination by the law.

Other forms of disability or long-term physical illness can make a person more likely to develop mental health problems, particularly depression.[55] Any illness or disability that restricts social contact or the ability to take part in activities outside the home is likely to put a person at risk of mental distress.[56]

People with epilepsy are at a higher risk of developing depression because of the stigma associated with the illness, as well as because of the impact of receiving a diagnosis of epilepsy.

There are specific problems associated with the onset of depression in people with learning disabilities who have limited means of communication. Carers of people with learning disabilities need to take notice of changes in behaviour that may indicate feelings of depression.[57]

Mental Health, Race and Ethnicity

One mistake we often make is to assume that people from black and minority ethnic (BME) backgrounds all share the same struggles with cultural difference. In fact, there are many differences within BME communities, just as there are between the majority white population and the other diverse cultures that live in Scotland.

The common factor BME communities in Scotland share is the experience of being treated as different and therefore experiencing stigma.

Evidence from England shows that:

- Much higher numbers of people from minority ethnic communities are subject to compulsory treatment orders

- African-Caribbean men have a 60% higher rate of depression than white people

- The incidence of attempted suicide and self-harm among young Asian women is higher than among their white counterparts

- Pakistani and Bangladeshi women have higher rates of common mental health problems (anxiety and depression) than white women.[58]

The *Equal Minds* report highlights the negative effects of racism on mental health. Within a twelve-month period, over three-fifths of people from visible minority groups and over one-half of minority white groups (for example from Eastern Europe, England or Ireland) had experienced property damage, physical assault or offensive remarks in a public place.

The term 'institutional racism' refers to the practices of large organisations that result in people from minority ethnic groups being treated unfairly. It does not mean that individual workers treat their colleagues or service users differently, although in some cases this does happen. Instead, it refers to policies and practices that create inequality. In mental health services, for instance, some of the assessment tools with which we are most familiar are based on a Western view of the world. One example would be the difficulty of translating the word 'depression' into South Asian languages.

We need to understand that concepts about mental health are different in different cultures – therefore we cannot assume that everyone shares the same ideas about mental health problems.

Black and Minority Ethnic Communities and Stigma

As part of a national commitment to mental health awareness-raising and tackling stigma, the Glasgow Anti-Stigma Partnership 'see me' and the National Resource Centre for Ethnic Minority Health published a research report, *Mosaics of Meaning*, in 2007. This work looks at the stigma associated with mental health problems within the five largest BME communities in Glasgow.

The project highlighted important findings around beliefs and attitudes, including:

- **Shame** is very strong in some communities. So much so, that family members keep mental health problems a secret, choosing instead to care for the individual in isolation. The reported value placed on family reputation may be such that the family will not discuss mental health problems even with a doctor. The higher the status of the family, the greater may be the reluctance to discuss the issue, regardless of educational achievement.

- **Marriage prospects** for people with mental health problems was reported as a major concern for the Muslim, Sikh, Hindu and African/Caribbean communities. This appears to be related to the notion of mental health problems 'being passed on in the blood'. Many community informants suggested that this provides a strong incentive for families to keep mental health problems a secret –

  > 'The main reason is to keep it a secret until they get married because the main thing is to get married'.

- **Black Magic or Spirits** were reported by all communities as a likely cause of mental health problems. Some cultures believe that mental health problems can be caused by possession by spirits or '*jinn*'. It was also reported that someone might put a curse on a person or a family to avenge a wrong and this could provoke mental disturbance. On the other hand, many Chinese people referred to causes of mental health problems as isolation and 'the pressures of life'.

> 'I remember my mum's uncle asking my mother what tablets I was taking and my mother told him that the tablets were for my arm and leg. But I was using antidepressants and sleeping tablets. She told him a little lie. Maybe if she had told him about this, my engagement would have broken down because my marriage was an arranged marriage. All my family know that I have depression but they didn't tell her and her part of the family. When the engagement broke up, my family and I separated from each other. They refused me and after that I tried to commit suicide.' [59]

Black and Minority Ethnic Communities – Care and Treatment

The *Mosaics of Meaning* report also highlights some important differences within BME communities regarding attitudes towards treatment for mental health problems.

- If **Muslims** believe that their problems are caused by bad spirits, they are likely to seek advice and support from their religious leaders.

- **Language barriers**, for those who are not confident speaking English, might also lead people to consult religious leaders as respected members of the community, and in whom they can most easily confide.

- **Young people** from Muslim and Chinese communities may be less likely to believe in spirits and more likely to view mental health problems as an illness. They will therefore tend to seek help from a GP.

- There are concerns around **confidentiality** when consulting doctors. Members of the Hindu and African or Caribbean communities in Glasgow expressed general distrust of doctors and social workers.

- Many South Asian patients believe in **several causes** rather than one single cause for their illnesses, and therefore use a number of treatments at the same time, e.g. traditional treatments and modern medications.

- **Religious solutions** may be sought by Indian families when mental health problems are assigned to 'divine wrath, a curse, black magic or karma of a previous life.' Treatment may include prayers and bathing in the temple tank.

- **Holistic approaches** to health treatment, where body and mind are regarded as one, are common in Chinese communities.

Refugees, Asylum Seekers and Mental Health

Contrary to some opinion, the majority of refugees and asylum seekers have moved to this country as a last resort – as a means to escape intolerable situations at home. This means that they have already experienced severe stress, and may be vulnerable to mental health problems. Refugees are likely to have experienced significant losses, e.g. loss of home, family, friends, profession, country, culture and hopes for the future. Once in Britain, they experience a further set of challenges and problems. These can include coping with multiple changes, making psychological and practical adjustments in an unfamiliar setting and having an uncertain future. Many may also face racism while trying to cope with unfamiliar cultural traditions.[60]

It is no surprise therefore, that the mental health of refugees and asylum seekers may be poor. Offering help may be difficult because many asylum seekers are fearful of anyone who may be able to influence their right to stay here and may not wish to reveal any vulnerability. The Scottish Refugee Council can offer help and guidance. Visit www.scottishrefugeecouncil.org.uk/advice

Mental Health and Gypsy or Traveller Communities

Gypsy and traveller people face specific challenges related to their health needs because of the nature of their travelling lifestyle. This is increased by the racism they experience because of peoples' views about their lifestyle choice. Health services in the UK are designed for people who are resident in one place for a set period, and it can therefore be difficult for gypsies and travellers to access services that require more than one appointment. The majority of health boards are making efforts to provide healthcare for gypsies and travellers, including specially trained health workers.

Racism is a particular stress for travelling people, especially when it is combined with a poor level of cultural understanding between travelling people and the rest of the population. This is made worse by a lack of understanding of the different types of gypsy and traveller groups in Scotland. False assumptions drive many of the negative responses.

Mental Health and Rurality

People in rural areas may experience isolation, and those in small communities may also feel that they have less privacy than their urban counterparts. Service planning may need to be particularly aware of issues around stigma.

Rural Scotland differs from the rest of Scotland but there are also differences within rural areas. Issues such as transport, access to education and health and social opportunities can impact on the wellbeing of rural communities.

Mental Health and Economic Migrants

The term 'economic migrant' refers to people who have moved to another country to improve their standard of living or to access better opportunities. Some people are deeply critical of the influx of economic migrants from other parts of Europe into Britain. However, they fail to remember the massive number of people who continue to emigrate from Britain to other countries for exactly the same reason. Migration is a common life choice and could be argued to be a basic human right.

Most people choose to migrate to another country in order to improve their life chances, but many do not take into account the impact of this on mental health. Living in another country, particularly one where the language spoken is different to one's native language, is very stressful and this stress can lead to mental health problems, especially in the first few months and years.

The World Health Organisation (WHO) has recommended that host countries ensure that mental health services are appropriate to immigrant groups. This includes making sure that help is available for migrants to integrate into the social and cultural life of the country, and that knowledge and training of health workers is appropriate and culturally sensitive.[61]

Mental Health and Religion or Belief

'Religion' and 'belief' are terms that encompass a rich and diverse experience of spirituality. They range from traditional religious practices to secular practices that recognise a spiritual dimension.

Spiritual practices include:

- Belonging to a faith tradition, and participating in associated community-based activities
- Ritual and symbolic practices or other forms of worship
- Pilgrimage and retreats
- Meditation and prayer
- Reading scripture
- Sacred music (listening to, singing and playing), including songs, hymns, psalms and devotional chants
- Acts of compassion (including work, especially teamwork)
- Deep reflection (contemplation)
- Yoga, Tai Chi and similar disciplined practices
- Engaging with and enjoying nature
- Contemplative reading (of literature, poetry, philosophy etc.)
- Appreciation of the arts, and engaging in creative activities
- Maintaining stable family relationships and friendships (especially those involving high levels of trust and intimacy)
- Group or team sports, recreational or other activities involving a special quality of fellowship.[62]

Evidence suggests that religious belief and spiritual practice are protective factors in maintaining positive mental health and promoting recovery. People who are committed to some form of spiritual practice or belief are less likely to die by suicide, experience depression or misuse substances. Where depression or other mental health problems do occur, religious belief or spiritual practice has been found to improve both the rate and the experience of recovery.[63]

The challenge to those committed to equality is to recognise the value of diversity and to make no assumptions or judgments about a person's belief system. Knowledge of the positive value of spiritual beliefs and practice means that in any setting committed to positive mental health, there should be both recognition and support of individuals' spiritual beliefs.

In a clinical setting, chaplains play a clear role in offering comfort and support to those who desire it. Chaplaincies should therefore represent a range of faiths and spiritual beliefs.

Those offering support to people experiencing distress may ask open questions to allow the person to discuss their spirituality. One example of such a question is 'What keeps you going in difficult times?'

Mental Health and Sexuality

'From an early age Lesbian, Gay, Bisexual and Transgendered (LGBT) people face a huge number of barriers, challenges and discrimination because of their sexual orientation or gender identity. Hiding such a significant part of their identity is one of the first things

133

many young LGBT people learn to do, which naturally impacts on self-identity and self-esteem.

Family disruption and rejection from the family home is a common experience for young LGBT people who reveal their identity in an unsupportive environment. Isolation from their peer group and significant levels of homophobic bullying, both verbal and physical, are also particular to the early experiences of young LGBT people.' [64]

People in the LGBT community are more likely to experience mental health problems than other groups and may be less willing to seek professional help. Anxiety, depression, self-harm, suicide and attempted suicide have all been linked with the combined effects of the experience of prejudice, discrimination, isolation and internalised negative feelings. Low self-esteem can be implicated in a wide range of health problems for LGBT people.

- From an early age, LGBT people face barriers, challenges and discrimination because of their sexual orientation or gender identity.

- Family disruption and rejection from the family home is a common experience for young LGBT people who reveal their identity in an unsupportive environment.

- Isolation from their peer group and significant levels of homophobic bullying, both verbal and physical, are also particular to the early experiences of young LGBT people.

- 'Gay' is now the most commonly used term of abuse in the school playground.

- Young LGBT people often leave school early and fail to meet their academic potential due to such negative experiences.[64]

Mental Health and Transgendered People

The term 'transgender' is an umbrella term referring to a person whose gender identity or gender expression falls outside of stereotypical gender norms. A transsexual person is one who was born as one gender and lives as the other. They may or may not have had surgical or hormonal intervention, may not be choosing to have such intervention or may be in a transition process.

The main issue for transsexual people is that they have experienced an increasing realisation that the gender in which they were born does not match their perception of themselves.

However, transgender is a much broader issue. There are people who do not define themselves as either gender, preferring to have a gender-neutral persona. This may cause confusion and stigma because the use of gender as a means of categorising people is central to many people's view of the social world.

Risks to mental health and wellbeing in people who are transgendered seem to be associated with the major life changes that such a transition brings about, as well as the difficulties of fitting into a society that is, at best, ignorant of transgendered issues and at worst, discriminatory.

Research into the mental health of transgendered people is very limited and tends to be linked to research into gay, lesbian and bisexual people. This may be inappropriate as the transgendered person may identify as heterosexual.[65]

Suicide leaves a painful legacy in the lives of the people it touches. The pain is often deepened by the same stigma and taboo that stifles open talk about suicide. Everyone's bereavement journey is different. People within a family or circle of friends will experience the suicide loss of the same loved one in their own way. Knowing about some commonly experienced feelings and thoughts may help this individual process.

After a suicide people may feel:

- **Alone:** Why do others avoid talking about suicide and stay away?

- **Sad:** I miss him or her … a tragic end to a troubled life.

- **Devastated:** How could it come to this?

- **Angry:** Why was so little support available?

- **Afraid:** Are these powerful feelings normal?

- **Ashamed:** How could this have happened to our family?

- **Guilty:** Did we do all we could?

- **Abandoned:** How could he or she have left me like this?

People's feelings vary and not all those named will be experienced by everyone. Some people will experience other feelings. Feelings are not right or wrong. They indicate where we are hurting and they can be helped by sharing them with people we trust.

Struggles after a suicide can include:

- **Disbelief:** Was it really suicide? It is so hard to accept.

- **Ambivalence:** She or he's no longer suffering, but I wish they had found a way to stay alive

- **Coping:** How can I get on with life while coming to terms with this suicide?

- **Review:** I go over and over what happened – sifting events and conversations

- **Searching:** How can I make sense of this and find meaning in the loss?

- **Renewal:** I'm seeking a way to move on, perhaps reviewing values and priorities.

Some people have thoughts of suicide themselves, and occasionally act on these thoughts.

Remember:

Tell people you trust about your thoughts, feelings and struggles – including thoughts you may have about self-harm or suicide.

Ask a person affected by suicide about the support they need and whether they have thoughts of suicide themselves.

Listen to the stories of the suicide bereaved – hear the pain, attend to the distress, and support the search for meaning in the loss.

Keep Safe from suicide while creating a safe place for people to share their sorrow and struggles, and to experience healing support.

Some keys to healing:

1. **Acknowledge the death and the suicide**: Accepting the reality of the death and the suicide will help the person heal.

2. **Attend to the pain and distress:** Taking time to experience, express and explore the pain of the loss helps heal the wounds, even though the scars may remain.

3. **Seek support and solitude:** People bereaved by suicide require sensitivity to the need for support and solitude – and to be able to seek and ask for what is needed.

4. **Give healing time:** Impatient advice says 'get over it'. But suicide is something people learn to live with rather than put behind them. Grief, like all wounds, heals from the inside out – and this takes time and patience.

5. **Take an active role in recovery:** Taking an active part in recovery is essential to the recovery message. This holds true for all kinds of loss and distress.

'Healing After a Suicide' has been adapted from suicideTALK, with the kind permission of LivingWorks. For more training information, visit www.chooselife.net

Cognitive Behavioural Therapy – A brief explanation

Cognitive behavioural therapy (CBT) is based on the idea that thoughts, feelings and behaviours all influence one another. If we change one part of the process that includes thinking, feeling and acting we can manage life and our problems more effectively.

Dr Chris Williams has developed a Five Areas Approach to cognitive behavioural therapy that recognises the fact that the majority of people experiencing anxiety or depression can identify more than one area of difficulty and that they can be helped to identify potentially helpful changes to these areas. Changing one area will inevitably influence the other areas.

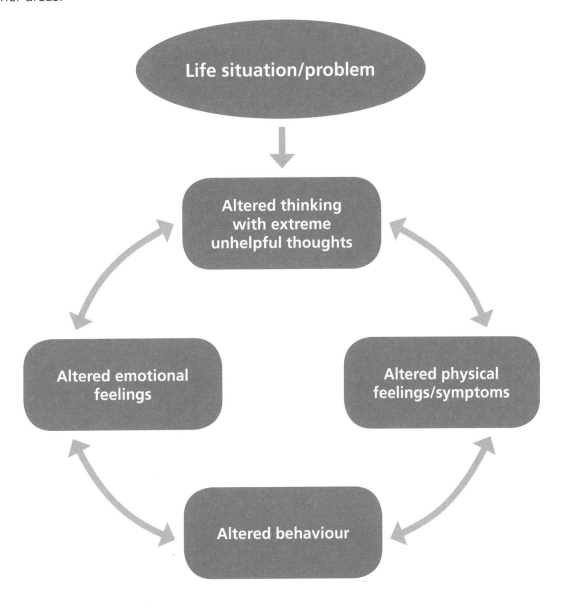

The idea of CBT is to encourage the person to think about each of the five areas and to identify unhelpful thoughts, feelings and behaviours that may be adding to the person's feelings of low mood or anxiety,

Once the person has identified the unhelpful behaviours, thoughts or feelings they have clear targets to focus on one step at a time.

Example

Mary has feelings of low mood and poor self esteem. With the help of a CBT online tool she realises that she has developed some unhelpful thinking that includes putting a negative spin on most situations in life (negative mental filter). She tends to notice the negative things that happen and not notice the positives so that if one thing goes wrong she will say things like: 'Today was awful. Everything went wrong.' She also realises that she has a negative view of how others see her, believing that her work colleagues think she is boring and stupid.

She is then encouraged to think about how her negative thinking impacts on her feelings. She says things like: 'I feel lonely at work because no-one likes me.'

The next step is to consider her altered behaviour. Mary admits to herself that she no longer goes out with her friends and does not take part in exercise classes that she used to enjoy. She also uses alcohol to reduce stress at the end of the day and eats more snack foods.

Once again Mary thinks about how these changes to her behaviour impact on her mood and her thinking. Without friends for support she feels even more lonely and using alcohol and snack food for comfort and not exercising as much means that she has put on some weight. This in turn makes her feel unhappy with her appearance and less likely to go out with friends.

Thinking about her mood, Mary becomes aware that she is more irritable than usual and that she doesn't enjoy any of her interests as much as before. She also feels ashamed of the way she looks and feels and is afraid that if her friends or family realised how bad she was feeling they would be angry with her or get impatient.

By looking at each of the areas, Mary gets a realistic picture of how her thinking and feelings are affecting her and also gives her the opportunity to work on these areas, one at a time.

Mary decides to work on the behavioural part of the five areas as a start. She asks one of her closest friends if she can join her at an exercise class and confides in her that she has been feeling very low recently and hasn't had the confidence to go the classes. Her friend is very understanding and offers to go with her to the class and to go for a coffee afterwards. They meet up in the car park so that Mary doesn't need to go in alone. After the class Mary's mood has improved and she finds she has enjoyed her friend's company. This encourages her to try changes to the other areas because she has recognised the way her behaviour has impacted on her mood.

This model and helpful resources for using it can be found on **www.llttf.com** Use of the website and its resources are free of charge and can be helpful to almost anyone.

1 WellScotland. *Scotland's Mental Health.* www.wellscotland.info/about/resources (accessed 17 November 2014)

2 RAMH http://ramh.org/about/ understanding-mental-health/

3 Department of Health. (2001). *Making it Happen: A Guide to Delivering Mental Health Promotion.*

4 Scottish Executive. (2003). *Mental Health Improvement: What works?*

5 Department of Health. (2006). *Mind Your Own Business.*

6 Department of Health. (2007). *Attitudes to Mental Illness in England.*

7 Becker, R., Meister, N., Storme, G. and Brondino, M. (1999). Employment Outcomes for Clients with Severe Mental Illness in a PACT Model Replication. *Psychiatric Service,* 50: 104–6.

8 see me Scotland. *Stigma Story: Jen.* www.seemescotland.org.uk (accessed 17 November 2014)

9 Rogers, A. and Pilgrim, D. (2003). *Mental Health and Inequalities.* Palgrave Macmillan, Basingstoke; Meltzer, D., Fryers, T. and Jenkins, R. (2004). *Social Inequalities and the Distribution of the Common Mental Disorders.* Psychology Press, Hove.

10 ISD Scotland. ISD *Practice Team Information.* (2007). www.isdscotland.org (accessed 17 November 2014)

11 Hafner, H. and An der Heiden, W. (1997). Epidemiology of Schizophrenia. *Canadian Journal of Psychiatry,* 42(2): 139–51.

12 Thornicroft, G. (1991). Social Deprivation and Rates of Treated Mental Disorder. Developing Statistical Models to Predict Psychiatric Service Utilisation. *British Journal of Psychiatry,* 158: 475–84.

13 NHS Health Scotland. (2007). *Establishing a Core Set of National, Sustainable Mental Health Indicators for Adults in Scotland: Rationale Paper.* www.healthscotland.com/ documents/2160.aspx

14 Gostin. (2001) cited in *World Health Organization et al.* (2004); Tidyman. (2004) cited in Myers et al. (2005).

15 Brown, W. and Kandirikirira, N. (2007). *Recovering Mental Health in Scotland: Report on Narrative Investigation of Mental Health Recovery.* Scottish Recovery Network, Glasgow.

16 Mental Health Foundation. (2006). *Cheers – Understanding the Relationship between Mental Health and Alcohol.* www.mentalhealth.org.uk/sites/ default/files/cheers_report.pdf (accessed 3 February 2016)

17 Rethink. *Why Cannabis Should Stay at Class C: The Impact of Cannabis.*

18 Seivewright, N., McMahon, C. and Egleston, P. (2005). Stimulant Use Still Going Strong: Revisiting… Misuse of Amphetamines and Related Drugs. *Advances in Psychiatric Treatment,* 11: 262–9.

19 Office for National Statistics. (2002). *Non-fatal Suicidal Behaviour among Adults 16 to 74 in Great Britain.* www.ons.gov.uk/ons/rel/psychiatric-morbidity/non-fatal-suicidal-behaviour-among-adults/aged-16-74-in-great-britain/index.html (accessed 17 November 2014)

20 Tribe, R. and Ravel, H. (Eds.) (2003). *Working with Interpreters in Mental Health.* Brunner-Routledge, East Sussex.

21 Outside the Box Development Support. (2008). *Adults' Experiences of Self-harm.* http://otbds.org/wp-content/uploads/2015/12/SH_final_report.pdf (accessed 3 February 2016)

22 Samaritans. (2007). *Understanding Self Injury.*

23 Glasgow Violence against Women Partnership. *Self-harm and Suicide amongst Black and Minority Women: A Conference Report* www.bemis.org.uk/PDF/Report%20on%20Self%20Harm%20and%20Suicide%20among%20Minority%20Ethnic%20Women.pdf (accessed 17 November 2014)

24 Coia, N., John, S., Dobbie, F., Bruce, S., McGranachan, M. and Simons, L. (2002). *Something to Tell You: A Health Needs Assessment of Young Gay, Lesbian and Bisexual People in Glasgow.* Greater Glasgow NHS Board, Glasgow.

25 National Institute for Clinical Excellence (NICE). *Depression: Management of Depression in Primary and Secondary Care: Clinical Guideline 23. (2007).*

26 TheSite. *MDMA.* www.thesite.org/drink-and-drugs/drugs-a-z/mdma-9989.html (accessed 3 February 2016

27 Kim H.L., Streltzer J. and Goebert D. (1999). St. John's Wort for Depression: A Meta-analysis of Well-defined Clinical Trials. *Journal of Nervous and Mental Disease,* 187: 532–8.

28 Linde K., Berner M.M. and Kriston L. (2008). *St John's Wort for Depression (Cochrane review).* The Cochrane Library, Chichester, UK. http://onlinelibrary.wiley.com/doi/10.1002/14651858.CD000448.pub3/pdf (accessed December 2014)

29 Blumenthal J.A., Babyak M.A. and Moore K. A., et al. (1999). Effects of Exercise Training on Older Patients with Major Depression. *Archives of Internal Medicine,* 159: 2349–56.

30 Tuunainen A., Kripke D.F. and Endo T. (2004). Light Therapy for Non-seasonal Depression (Cochrane Review). The Cochrane Library, Chichester, UK.

31 Campbell, C. et al. (1999). *Social Capital and Health.* London School of Economics.

32 Luo H., Meng F., Jia Y. and Zhao X. (1998). Clinical Research on the Therapeutic Effect of the Electro-acupuncture Treatment in Patients with Depression. *Psychiatry and Clinical Neurosciences,* 52: S338–40.

33 Field T.M. (1998). Massage Therapy Effects. *American Psychologist,* 53: 1270–81.

34 Murphy G.E., Carney R.M. and Knesevich M.A., et al. (1995). Cognitive Behaviour Therapy, Relaxation Training and Tricyclic Antidepressant Medication in the Treatment of Depression. Psychological Reports, 77: 403–20

35 Janakiramaiah N., Gangadhar B.N., Naga Venkatesha Murthy P.J., Harish M.G., Subbakrishna D.K. and Vedamurthachar A. (2000). *Antidepressant Efficacy of Sudarshan Kriya Yoga (SKY) in Melancholia: A Randomized Comparison with Electroconvulsive Therapy (ECT) and Imipramine.* Journal of Affective Disorders, 57: 255–9.

36 Churchill R., Hunot V., Corney R., Knapp M., McGuire H., Tylee A. and Wessely S. (2001). A Systematic Review of Controlled Trials of the Effectiveness and Cost-effectiveness of Brief Psychological Treatments for Depression. *Health Technology Assessment*, 5(35):1–173

37 The Royal College of Psychiatrists. *Mental Health and Growing Up, Third Edition: Depression in Children and Young People.* www.rcpsych.ac.uk/healthadvice/parentsandyouthinfo/youngpeople/depressioninyoungpeople.aspx (accessed 18 November 2014)

38 Mental Health Foundation. (1999). *Anxiety: Information.* www.mentalhealth.org.uk/a-to-z/a/anxiety (accessed 3 February 2016)

39 Silove, D., Sinnerbrink, I., Field, A., Manicavasagar, V. and Steel, Z. (1997). Anxiety, Depression and PTSD in Asylum-seekers: Assocations with Pre-migration Trauma and Post-migration Stressors. *The British Journal of Psychiatry,* 170: 351–7.

40 Mental Health Foundation. *Anxiety.* www.mentalhealth.org.uk/a-to-z/a/anxiety (accessed 3 February 2016)

41 The Scottish Government. *Scottish Advisory Committee on Drug Misuse: Psychostimulant Working Group Report.* www.gov.scot/Publications/2002/08/15141/9088 (accessed 3 February 2016)

42 Mind. (2007). *Understanding the Psychological Effects of Street Drugs.* www.mind.org.uk/media/859563/understanding-the-mental-health-effect-of-street-drugs-2014.pdf (accessed 18 November 2014)

43 Edwards, J. and McGorry, P.D. (2002). *Implementing Early Intervention in Psychosis.* Martin Dunitz, London.

44 Morrison A., Renton J.C., French P. and Bentall R. (2008) *Think You're Crazy? Think Again: A Resource Book for Cognitive Therapy for Psychosis.* Routledge, New York.

45 Arsenault, L., Cannon, M., Witton, J. and Murray, R.M. (2004). Casual association between cannabis and psychosis: examination of the evidence. *British Journal of Psychiatry,* 184: 110–17.

46 Royal College of Psychiatrists. *Severe Mental Illness (Psychosis).* www.rcpsych.ac.uk/expertadvice/youthinfo/parentscarers/disorders/psychosis.aspx (accessed 18 November 2014)

47 Walsh, E., Moran, P., Scott, C. et al. (2003). Prevalence of Violent Victimisation in Severe Mental Illness. *British Journal of Psychiatry,* 183: 233–8.

48 Pharoah F., Mari J., Rathbone J. and Wong W. (2010). *Family Intervention for Schizophrenia,* Cochrane Database of Systematic Reviews 2, CD000088.

49 The Royal College of Psychiatrists. *Schizophrenia.* www.rcpsych.ac.uk/mentalhealthinformation/mentalhealthproblems/schizophrenia/schizophrenia.aspx (accessed 18 November 2014)

50 National Collaborating Centre for Mental Health. (2006). *Bipolar Disorder Management of Bipolar Disorder in Adults, Children and Adolescents in Primary and Secondary Care.* www.rcpsych.ac.uk/ files/samplechapter/BipolarSCx.pdf (accessed 18 November 2014)

51 Dahlgren G. and Whitehead M. (1991). *Policies and Strategies to Promote Social Equity in Health.* Institute for Futures Studies, Stockholm.

52 Age Concern and Mental Health Foundation. (2006). *Promoting Mental Health and Well-being in Later Life: A First Report from the UK Inquiry into Mental Health and Well-being in Later Life.* www. ageuk.org.uk/Documents/EN-GB/ For-professionals/Care/Mental%20 Health%20and%20Wellbeing%20 in%20later%20life_pro. pdf?dtrk=true (accessed 3 February 2016)

53 Age UK. (2008). *Discussing depression with your GP.* www.ageuk.org.uk/documents/ en-gb/discussing_depression_with_ your_gp_adv.pdf?dtrk=true (accessed December 2014)

54 Age Concern. (2007) *Promoting Mental Health and Well-Being in Later Life.* www.apho.org.uk/ resource/view.aspx?RID=70414 (accessed 3 February 2016)

55 MacHale, S. (2002). Managing Depression in Physical Illness. *Advances in Psychiatric Treatment,* 8: 297–305.

56 Royal College of Psychiatrists. (2007). *Physical Illness and Mental Health.* www.rcpsych.ac.uk/ healthadvice/problemsdisorders/ copingwithphysicalillness.aspx (accessed 18 November 2014)

57 Royal College of Psychiatrists. (2001). *Depression in People with Learning Disability.* www.rcpsych.ac.uk/pdf/ Depression%20ld%20final.pdf (accessed 18 November 2014)

58 Scottish Executive. National Programme for Improving Mental Health and Well-being. *Addressing Mental Health Inequalities in Scotland: Equal Minds.* www.scotland.gov.uk/ Publications/2005/11/04145113 /51135 (accessed 18 November 2014)

59 NHS Health Scotland. (2008). *Are you really listening? Stories about Stigma, Discrimination and Resilience amongst BME Communities in Scotland.* www.healthscotland.com/ uploads/documents/19864-Are%20 you%20really%20listening.pdf (accessed 18 November 2014)

60 Tribe, R. (2002). The Mental Health of Refugees and Asylum Seekers. *Advances in Psychiatric Treatment,* 8: 240–8.

61 World Health Organization. Global Consultation on Migrant Health. 3–5 March 2010. www.who.int/hac/ events/2_migrant_sensitive_health_ services_22Feb2010.pdf (accessed December 2014)

62 Royal College of Psychiatrists. (2006). *Spirituality and Mental Health.* www.rcpsych.ac.uk/ mentalhealthinformation/therapies/ spiritualityandmentalhealth.aspx (accessed 18 November 2014)

63 Rethink. (2005). *Spirituality and Mental Illness: Information leaflet.* www.rethink.org/living-with-mental- illness/wellbeing-physical-health/ spirituality (accessed 3 February 2016)

64 Stonewall Scotland and NHS
   Scotland. (2003). *Towards a Healthier
   LGBT Scotland.*
   http://uprainbowpride.com/
   downloads/Stonewall%20Report.pdf
   (accessed 3 February 2016)

65 Mind. (2004). *Understanding
   Gender Dysphoria.*
   www.mentalhealthintheuk.co.uk/
   Understandinggenderdysphoria.pdf
   (accessed 18 November 2014)